Spongeware

1835  1935

Makers, Marks, and Patterns

Henry E. Kelly
Arnold A. & Dorothy E. Kowalsky

Schiffer® Publishing Ltd

4880 Lower Valley Road, Atglen, PA 19310 USA

To Douglas Leishmen

Library of Congress Cataloging-in-Publication Data

Kelly, Henry E.
Spongeware 1835-1935 : makers, marks, and patterns / Henry E. Kelly, Arnold A. & Dorothy E. Kowalsky.
p. cm.
SBN 0-7643-1270-7 (alk. paper)
1. Sponged ware. I. Kowalsky, Arnold A. II. Kowalsky, Dorothy E. III. Title.
NK4340.S65 K45 2001
738.3'7--dc21
00-011720

Designed by Bonnie M. Hensley
Cover design by Bruce M. Waters
Type set in Zapf Chancery Bd BT/Zapf Humanist BT

ISBN: 0-7643-1270-7
Printed in China
1 2 3 4

Published by Schiffer Publishing Ltd.
4880 Lower Valley Road
Atglen, PA 19310
Phone: (610) 593-1777; Fax: (610) 593-2002
E-mail: Schifferbk@aol.com
Please visit our web site catalog at **www.schifferbooks.com**

In Europe, Schiffer books are distributed by Bushwood Books
6 Marksbury Avenue Kew Gardens
Surrey TW9 4JF England
Phone: 44 (0) 20-8392-8585; Fax: 44 (0) 20-8392-9876
E-mail: Bushwd@aol.com
Free postage in the UK. Europe: air mail at cost.

Contents

Acknowledgments

We have been greatly helped in the compilation of this book by many people. I wish to thank the staffs of the following museums: the Hunterian Museum of the University of Glasgow, The Ulster Folk and Transport Museum, the Highland Folk Museum at Kingussie in Highland Region, Scotland, and Fochabers Museum. Collectors and friends are too numerous to mention in total. However, Sandra Aldridge, Dr. John and Rosa Baker, Tessa Bennett, John Birdsey, Sandra Deas, Alex Dufour of the Brixton Pottery, Amy Earls, Michael and Marlene Egan, Pauline Jamieson, George Kearney, Douglas Leishman, Niall McKelvie, Elizabeth Mosse, and Margaret West must be mentioned, as well as many others who have lent us pieces or allowed us to photograph them. Several American and English auction houses have been very helpful in providing catalogues and photographs and I should like here to express my thanks to Dreweatt Neate of Donnington in Berks, who provided the beautiful photograph for Figure 2, Garth's Auctions of Delaware, Ohio, Horst Auctioneers of Ephrata, Pennsylvania, Alderfer auction Co. of Hatfield, Pennsylvania, Pook & Pook Inc. of Downingtown, Pennsylvania, Skinner of Boston, Massachusetts, and Ken Farmer, Auctions and Estates of Radford, Virginia.

To all who have let us use their pieces or their photographs, mentioned or unmentioned, we should like here to express our thanks.

A Brief Word About the Pricing in This Book

Prices reflected are current, retail both here in the United States and the United Kingdom, and are for pieces in extremely fine condition with no repairs, chips or hairlines. Although the prices are subjective, they are given in both pounds (sterling) and in U.S. dollars. To take into account the fluctuations in the pound's values in relation to U.S. dollars, U.S. dollar values are double the pound amount.

Preface — The Inception of this Book

This book came about from two sources. One of the authors (Henry E. Kelly) has had an interest in Spongeware for many years and has, in fact, published a booklet on the subject with particular reference to his native Scotland which played a crucial role in the origin of the ware. The other author (Arnold A. Kowalsky) has a great interest in the backstamps that told about the origin of pieces, and has also published on the subject. The two were in regular correspondence when Arnold Kowalsky acquired a large collection of photographs of Spongeware, which had been assembled by Mr. Durrie before his death. As the photographs were several hundred in number, this seemed like a good opportunity to Arnold to produce a serious book on the subject; especially as Henry had also been collecting photographs and was able to increase both the number and scope of the illustrations.

Mr. Durrie had intended to write a book to accompany the photographs. Unfortunately, his studies had not advanced far enough to make possible the publication of his notes. A decision was made by Henry and Arnold to write an extended text and add selected marks. This is what has been done. Henry E. Kelly has known the Durrie collection only from black and white copies, which sometimes led to uncertainties, particularly about color. (For instance, Mr. Durrie seems to have disregarded the distinction between crimson and red). In general, the difficulties have not been insurmountable.

The Durrie photographs have added to the authors' corpus of knowledge on the subject. They have provided a great deal of information on the subject of what was made for the American market by English potters (and a few Scots and Dutchmen). This in itself is very interesting since, on the other side of the 49th parallel, the Scots potteries seem to have been of much more importance than the English. While one says "English," it is probable that one could substitute the word "Staffordshire" without too much inaccuracy. Apart from Church Gresley, very few non-Staffordshire potteries seem to be represented in the Durrie collection. At the same time, it is essential to remember that a very large proportion of spongeware is not marked and is almost impossible to assign to a specific pottery or even to a specific country.

It is important to remember also that American collectors have bought pieces from many countries to enhance their collections, and Durrie was no exception. Unfortunately, it is obvious that he did not always know where the pieces were originally found. When he knew the origin, the information can be startling — as with the rice dish that came from Persia, a market about which we were, and are, totally ignorant. The study of commercial relations between British potters and the American market is still in its infancy (like the study of spongeware). Too many people still ignore the importance of spongeware, and scorn the study of the late nineteenth century, for progress to be made. Perhaps our entry into the twenty-first century will make the nineteenth seem more distant and more worthy of study.

Introduction

For over one hundred and fifty years spongeware has brought color and enjoyment into the lives of people all over the world, from the humblest to those of some means. On the vast prairies of North America and Central Asia, on remote islands such as St. Kilda where poverty and isolation dominated lives, in the jungles of Borneo, and the teeming cities of India, spongeware was known and treasured. So popular was it in the Indonesian islands that pieces were used to decorate the exteriors of temples and palaces as well as more ordinary buildings. In more modern times collectors in the U.S.A. and Canada, in Great Britain and Holland, in Malaysia and South Africa amongst other places, some of them people of considerable wealth, have learned to love this ware and collect it with great pleasure. So popular has it become that studio potters, and even some commercial firms, have started to produce modern versions of the old ware.

On the other hand, the serious study of spongeware is of very recent growth and is still in its infancy. There are two main reasons for this. First there is an inherent difficulty in that spongeware was seldom marked. It was aimed, for the most part, at the lower end of the market, the body was coarse and the workers unskilled and frequently careless. This meant that, although it was bread and butter for many potteries, they were ashamed of making it and sometimes tried to conceal the fact. Then, too, certain patterns persisted for many years and were very difficult to date because of this.

The second difficulty lies in the terminology used by early writers on the subject. The word spatterware became associated with spongeware in the U.S.A. and this somehow stuck. Early books on the subject, as well as some of the later ones, seem to be talking about three or four decorating techniques at the same time, thus completely confusing the subject. All four techniques (brushstroke, spattering, sponge printing, and splash glazing) were used, sometimes in combination, to produce colorful wares that were greatly prized by Americans and Canadians in the nineteenth century.

Brushstroke, spattering and dabbing were all techniques used in the eighteenth century and continued into the nineteenth. Compared with them, sponge-printing came onto the scene late in time. The evidence is not conclusive, but the origins seem to be in Scotland about the year 1835. The earliest indications of manufacture that are in print all point to that country. Many of the most primitively decorated sherds have turned up in Scotland, particularly in Bo'ness and Glasgow. Silesia, an area variously in Germany or Poland depending on date, claims an early incidence of sponge-printing. This seems to be an unsupported claim though spongeware was (and is) undoubtedly made in large quantities in that area.

The first technique employed is **'brushstroke'** or **'hand painting'**. This was the application of color by the use of a brush (often called a pencil by potters), usually to the biscuit body by a fair but not too highly skilled worker. The painter could be working on china or on earthenware. The painter of the former was usually the more skilled and the more highly paid. The job was awarded on skill rather than on sex, though earthenware was most often worked on by 'paintresses'.

The second technique is **spattering**. This consisted of the application of color, usually to the biscuit body, as a dry powder or a powder mixed with oil. It was frequently blown onto the body by a skilled workman using some sort of pipe. (Picture 1) There is a widely held misconception that spattering was painted dot by dot using a very small brush. The expense of decoration in this mode would have meant the pieces were aimed at the millionaire market. As it is, spattering produced a relatively expensive ware, quite unrelated to spongeware. **The most common use for the spattering technique was in putting one or more colors in a deep border around a dish that had a brushstroke bird or flower in the center. It seems best to avoid confusion by limiting the term spatterware to dishes of this description, and completely avoiding the word in connection with sponge printing, where it is completely inappropriate.** (Picture 2). It should be borne in mind, though, that these dishes are almost never truly "spattered;" the color is usually applied by dabbing with an ordinary sponge. The use of the term spatterware is, thus, a misnomer. This is unimportant so long as it is realized that this is so and that the use of the word spatter is otherwise confined to the genuine technique. In fact spatterware and sponge-printed ware can have had very little connection except in use, since spatterware seems to have been going out of production as spongeware was first being brought into use. Perhaps one displaced the other as being just as colorful but cheaper to produce.

DIFFERENTIATING TRUE SPATTERWARE FROM DABBING/SPATTERWARE

Picture 1. **Bonbonnaire**. 7.25" (18.5 cm). Pink ground spattered in blue with brushstroke flowers in blue gold and green. Mark: B.P. Co. Ltd. for Britannia Pottery Glasgow. c. 1930. This is true **spattering** and, as can be seen, is quite different from the coloring in "spatterware." £40, $80.

Picture 2. **Plate**. Painted in red, yellow and blue with a central cockerel in a landscape. The foliage is indicated by pink **dabbing**. A blue line. No mark. This is the type of ware generally called spatterware, a term which is inaccurate but generally accepted. £300, $600.

The third technique involves the use of an ordinary bath sponge dipped in color and applied to the biscuit body. It is the technique mentioned above in describing 'spatterware'. It is often found on delft, certainly as early as the eighteenth century and can be and has been confused with spattering. Probably the simplest term to use for this would be **dabbed ware,** the technique appears not to have attracted much in the way of literature. In fact, it is ignored by most of the American writers on spongeware, and is frequently described as spatter. It can certainly be easily confused with spattering on the one hand and with primitive sponge printing on the other but is, nevertheless, a separate and important technique. It is this confusion of spattering and dabbing with early attempts at sponge printing that has led to the inappropriate vocabulary used in the U.S.A. This has, in turn, cut American collectors off from those in the rest of the world.

The fourth technique, and the main subject of this book, is **sponge printing**. The ware is often referred to in Britain simply as spongeware, sometimes as sponge printed ware. A piece of the uncommercial ' root' of the sponge was cut into a shape either by the department foreman or by a specialist firm who sold ready-made sponges to potteries. The cut sponge was then fixed onto a wooden handle. Young, unskilled girls were provided with these along with some color on a saucer, a sherd, or a piece of leather. They sat in front of the biscuit ware that was on a turntable and applied the pattern just like a child making a potato print. A sponge is, of course, an animal and has no root but the word is used here to describe the hardest part of the sponge which fixes the sponge to a rock and is removed from the sponge before it is sold commercially.

This last technique was used on the coarsest, cheapest ware, sent out to the colonies, distributed in country districts round the potteries by traveling hawkers or peddlers, and in cities by the rag and bone man who exchanged the pots for old unwanted goods, clothing, or metals, etc. Its marketing was very different from goods using the other techniques, and was more likely to be in company with mocha ware and other slipwares in the hawker's basket. This is beautifully depicted in a painting by Miles Birket Foster in the Ulster Museum, showing a girl selling her pottery wares on a country road to cottage dwellers.

It seems worthwhile here to discuss the terms used in the U.S.A. by some collectors since they are both unique and very unhelpful. There seem to be four terms in frequent use: **spatter, design spatter, stick spatter,** and **cut sponge**. These terms are used to cover spatterware, dabbed ware and spongeware. In fact, the confusion has become so great that in one recently published book the terms spongeware and spatterware are used interchangeably to cover all of the above as well as splash glazes! (Splash glazing refers to the use of several different coloured glazes on a piece in patches. It was used initially as a way to conceal faults in the body but became quite popular on its own, especially on country wares. Green, brown, and blue with white [or cream when glazed over] were the most popular colours.)

The confusion seems to have arisen from the failure to realize that what is usually referred to as spatterware in fact actually displays dabbing with an ordinary sponge. The Robackers seem to have realized this and go on to use the term spatterware for both. This is quite legitimate so long as the term is confined to 'spatterware' border items with painted centerpieces. But Robacker then seems to get confused and sees in what he calls 'design spatter' dots of color. If a piece of this "design spatter" is examined closely it will be seen that the color does not consist of separate dots but of areas of color interrupted by dots of uncolored body. There are also blobs of intense color within the areas of color. In fact, what we have is exactly what you get if you dab something roughly with an ordinary sponge dipped in color. What Robacker has designated 'design spatter' is simply sponge printing using a more loosely textured sponge than is normal. This could indicate an early date, or a preferred texture, or a use of a cheaper part of the sponge. What it does not indicate is a difference of technique. In fact the technique of production is exactly the same and the density of the sponge varies continuously so that the use of the term is unhelpful and purely subjective.

In addition, Robacker invented the phrase 'flowing spatter' for a technique which is simply an early use of loosely textured sponge cut in an indeterminate shape and used to apply the color to the ware. This technique was used during the early manufacture of spongeware in Scotland. It seems to have become very popular in the U.S.A. where it had a much longer life than elsewhere. However, as it has no connection with spattering and does not flow, the choice of a name seems less than helpful.

Stick spatter is a curious term to use for a process that does not include spatter, uses no sticks, and is adequately covered by the term **'cut sponge'** or **'sponge-printing,'** which are the terms used in all the other English-speaking countries of the world. It is interesting that Robacker himself repudiated the term in his last book (Robacker). It seems best to keep the word spatter for spatterware and spongeware for the rest. It also seems best to realize that these techniques are very tenuously related and that perhaps it would be best to keep the subjects of spatterware and spongeware completely separate, especially since their association has led to a confused understanding of the subjects. The danger is seen in the book referred to above (Slesin et al.) which, in spite of having some of the loveliest illustrations ever made of spongeware, conveys no useful information!

A third difficulty is that the spread of the technique was fast, covered a very large area and many languages. Scotland, England and Holland were major producers, but many other countries were involved in manufacture with much of the known world its destination. Each area seems to study its own production as if it were an isolated phenomenon. American and English writers seem to know nothing of Scottish producers; southeast Asian writers seem to think that Holland was the only producer and no one seems to know much about export to Australia or South America or about the Japanese manufacturers.

It was certainly from Scotland that the technique was introduced into England where it was made by most whiteware potteries north of Bristol. Although the invention dates only from about 1835, the Adams Pottery in Stoke seems to have been manufacturing it in developed form somewhere around 1845. It probably was introduced to the Beleek Pottery from Glasgow. Its penetration into Wales, Holland and other European countries is undocumented, but not hard to imagine since there was constant intercourse between European and British potteries with much imitation in both directions. It probably came to North America by emigration. It was certainly present in prerevolutionary Russia. Sherds marked Kuznietsoff in the old, pre-revolutionary Cyrillic alphabet are attested to by Arlene and Paul Greaser (see Annotated Bibliography) and are still to be found in the flea markets of New York; presumably brought by immigrants. One of the oddest phenomena is the production of spongeware in Japan. The technique possibly reached Japan through export by European producers to southeast Asia. Only a few pieces of Japanese ware are known to have come from Sri Lanka and Indonesia so it is difficult to reach any meaningful conclusion on the subject. The technique seems to have been seldom used in southern Europe (or indeed anywhere except the Northern Hemisphere) until modern times. Although of little importance, an exception is to be seen in the International Museum of Ceramiques in Faenza, Italy, which exhibits one or two pieces of late majolica with fairly crude sponge-printed designs.

Throughout the nineteenth century up and even on into the twentieth until about 1930 spongeware was made in Scotland, England, Wales, Ireland, Holland, Belgium, France, Germany, Italy, Poland, Russia, Japan and the U.S.A. Its popularity, though, cannot be measured even in such global terms. Both Britain and Holland were at the head of empires that stretched throughout the globe. Wherever spongeware has been studied it can be traced back to British and Dutch manufacturers. In South Africa and Namibia, in India and Sri Lanka, in Myanmar (Burma), Malaysia and Indonesia it has been reported in enormous quantities and the principal manufacturers are always British and Dutch. In South Africa, along with hand painted wares, it was known as Boerenbont, a term that seems to mean something like "farmers fancy." This term, being Dutch, has been adopted in Indonesia. In Canada it was thought at first to have been a local manufacture and was known as Portneuf Pottery. This is now known, however, to have been largely Scottish and wholly British in origin so that the term Portneuf has become meaningless, though it is still used by dealers.

It should be pointed out, however, that very few samples of spongeware will be marked. It was the cheapest of wares and not considered worth marking. Indeed, some potteries were ashamed of manufacturing it and did not want it known that they were reduced to making anything so tawdry; particularly as some of them made it only when times were bad. Again, the people who used spongeware the most were seldom in a position to order new pieces to match old ones. They would not be interested in the maker so it was a waste of effort to mark the ware, especially since the workers were on piecework rates and would not be anxious to incur an extra task which would slow down production. The body used was a coarse type of earthenware. One recipe for a "common body," published in *The Pottery Gazette* for September 1, 1883, gives the following ingredients: 30 parts blue clay, 11 of flint, 13 of common clay and 5 and a half of stone. Perhaps most potteries used something like this for spongeware. Exceptions to this rule seem to be Adams of Stoke and the Links Pottery of Kirkcaldy, both of whom made carefully decorated spongeware with painted elements for export as a major part of their output and marked their wares fairly often. Methven's Links Pottery made a great deal of unmarked spongeware. Some pieces made for assured sources were very carefully marked, though not with the name of the Pottery. Nisbet Ware was destined for a china dealer in Edinburgh, Airlie Ware for one in Kirriemuir and Auld Heather Ware was destined for the American market. One lot was delayed due to a strike action and was dumped on the home market. As a result Auld Heather Ware can be found in Scotland. It should be emphasized that the three named wares all came on the scene fairly late, during what must have been already a fairly long period of manufacture of spongeware but probably after the initiation of Methven's export range. Lomond Ware, which is very similar to the above, is said to have been decorated independently in Kirkcaldy with the blanks bought from various sources.

Since ready-made sponges could be bought in by the potteries and since potters were extraordinarily mobile, the use of certain motifs cannot usually be taken as evidence of place of origin for pieces and all attribution of them that were based on such a foundation should be taken with a grain of salt. This makes the attribution of spongeware generally very difficult. Though occasionally pieces can be attributed on the basis of the shape of the piece and marked pieces are found from time to time. Several such pieces will be illustrated in this book. Otherwise, the surest footing for attribution would seem to be the complete coincidence of a pattern. Though, even here, there are pitfalls in attribution — as will be seen later.

In the earliest period of production colors used most often were blue and red, though various shades of green are also found. In Scotland purple and brown became very popular, with both colors gaining ground in England. Pink, yellow and other shades were introduced, but these remained less popular. Black became fairly common especially in Scotland. In the 1870s gray became by far the commonest color on spongeware and, in fact, is the most usual color in which we find the commonest named spongeware pattern — Grecian. This pattern is said to have been based on a Spode pattern that was, in turn, based on a Chinese pattern. Neither, however, has been illustrated in extant literature. Whatever its origins, and no matter whether it is found as a sponge-print or as a transfer-print, the pattern is now indecipherable and is, in fact, sometimes only a blur. It is found in dark blue, light blue, black, red and pink. However, gray is the overwhelmingly most common color. Although marked pieces are known from most Scottish and some English potteries, thousands of unmarked pieces are unattributable. Many American potteries that produced spongeware seem to have deliberately kept to the more primitive type of sponge motif, soft-edged and indeterminate in shape.

In its earliest phase sponge printing occurred by itself in rather indeterminate forms of dots, circles and other rather shapeless motifs. There is no attempt to imitate any external objects and the cutting was so soft-edged as sometimes to be confused with dabbing. This type of decoration seems to have continued with American country potteries over a long period of time and is well illustrated in McConnell. Early on, some English potteries experimented with sponge-printed borders on pieces with a central transfer-print. This experiment did not last, even though, as a technique, it seems to have been revived during the late nineteenth century as pieces for the American market, particularly the well known "rabbit plates." By 1870 sponge printing was fully developed. Sponges were now hard-edged and began to represent objects from ordinary life. Flowers, birds, mammals and insects were particularly popular, but many motifs are found, sometimes even humans. Dogs, cats, and even tigers and lizards have been seen. Cows became particularly popular in Scotland. There is even one instance known of a jockey jumping his horse over a fence. This was made either in Bells' Pottery or Britannia, both of Glasgow. The unmarked sherd was found in a mixed dump of spoilers. Around 1900 mottoes became very popular, particularly on the bottom of bowls' interiors with decoration in green and red, sometimes in combination with an animal sponge.

Another extension of skill was in large multicolored prints. Sponges for these pieces were made by tying two or more sponge 'roots' tightly together and carving them into a more complex pattern than was possible with a single sponge 'root'. These landscapes, baskets of flowers, etc. were then printed using several colors. This latter technique was also used occasionally on single sponges. In either case this must have required rather more skill on the part of the pottery girl than simple sponge printing in one color, since the different areas must have been given the different colors separately.

For the home market and the Canadian market the Scottish potteries mostly produced bowls from which porridge, broth and other foods were generally eaten by the working population. Plates, pitchers, cups, saucers, spit pots for invalids and many other forms were also produced. English potteries certainly produced bowls for the American market. Many plates and tea sets as well as child's tea sets were also sent across the Atlantic to the American market. The body on which the sponge printing was done was generally fairly coarse, though there are exceptions to this rule.

In the 1880s a new development in sponge-printing greatly changed the scope and nature of the ware. Throughout their lives some of the larger potteries in Britain and Holland produced spongeware that was more carefully manufactured than usual. It would appear that these potters were looking for other and more lucrative markets. The Links Pottery of Kirkcaldy, Fife, for instance, marked the spongeware that was destined for certain regular customers or for certain markets. These wares date from the twentieth century. Copeland seems to have had a flourishing export trade to India.

In the 1880s, however, Bells' Glasgow Pottery, the Links Pottery (often referred to as Methven's), the Société Cêramique of Maastricht in Holland, and Adams and George Jones of Stoke began to produce large rice dishes and soup plates for the southeast Asian market. These were decorated with sponge printing alone or with sponge printing combined with hand painted motifs. Société Cêramique was the successor of the Sphinx Pottery of Petrus Regout, which was earlier involved. These pieces were exported to an enormous area stretching from the Indian Peninsula to Borneo. Copeland also exported large amounts to the same area, though their products were rather different in design. Pieces sent to Asia by the first six potteries mentioned here were on a much better body than usual for spongeware. The decoration was much more carefully done, and certainly was not the work of an unskilled little girl. Little of this ware survived in Britain but of late much of it has begun to return from India, Sri Lanka, Malaysia and various parts of Indonesia. Illustrations of other pieces have been published in Burma.

Potteries other than those mentioned exported to this region, especially Verreville, Britannia and the Victoria Pottery, all of Glasgow, as well as several of the smaller Staffordshire potteries, the Bridgeness Pottery and Bo'ness Pottery. These, however, seem to have played a lesser part and in the case of the Bo'ness Pottery, at least, the slight returns could have been merely goods taken out by British families for their own use. The Glasgow Pottery of J. & M. P. Bell & Co. Ld. backed up their spongeware export to the area with a series of transfer prints specially designed by Chinese artists. This spongeware had an enormous success and is still found in large quantities in collections in both Britain and Southeast Asia.

The strangest fact about the spongeware of the "Big Six" (Bell, Methven, Adams, Jones, Sphinx, Société Cêramique) is that they are virtually indistinguishable from each other. They made the same patterns in the same color schemes, and it is impossible without marks to say who made which piece or who originated a pattern and who copied it. The truth is that all six copied from each other in an attempt to keep their share of the market. However, the Scottish potteries made one type of spongeware which was very popular in the home market as well as in the export trade. This was **Scottish flow blue**. This type of decoration appears on the interior of deep bowls, on soup plates, dinner plates, and porringers, both on outer and inner faces. It consisted of painted plant forms in blue that covered most of the piece but had a sponge-printed border also in blue. In firing the whole decoration was encouraged to flow through the glaze in an almost uncontrolled way so that the entire surface was covered to some extent in blue. In the most extreme cases, the pattern is almost lost in flown color. It was immensely popular at home and was made by a number of potteries and frequently marked. Curiously the mark in Scotland, at least, seldom identifies the manufacturer to the uninitiated since it is usually a black sponge-printed symbol. Verreville Pottery used a Dog of Fo or a bugle, the Links Pottery used an elephant and both they and Bells' seem to have used a St. Andrew's Saltire with its cross made up of the word Bulloch, for a Rangoon firm for which the pieces were often made. Scotland had no monopoly on this type of ware, but it certainly seems to have been more popular in Scotland than elsewhere.

Another characteristic of the latter part of the nineteenth century is the appearance of the **'Irish Potato Bowl'**. These are large bowls with an everted rim. I have given this title of convenience to the bowl, since every time I have seen one on sale the dealer has told me 'It came from Ireland originally' or 'It's a potato bowl like they use in Ireland'. Certainly they occur in Ireland with greater frequency than in Britain, and Irish collections often have matching pairs or even trios, a phenomenon not known with any frequency in Britain or elsewhere. The only Irish pottery that could have made these bowls would have been Beleek, but neither the body nor the decoration agrees with known pieces from this pottery. The most likely origin for them is somewhere in Scotland, which would be consistent with their style. There is also the possibility that some of them, at least, are English in origin. They often have complex, multicolored sponge prints which date them to the end of the nineteenth or the beginning of the twentieth century. There is no recorded instance of a marked potato bowl.

The subject of attribution to Irish potteries is very important since dealers often claim these potato bowls to be of Irish manufacture. The only potteries that fall within the correct period for making spongeware and whiteware are Beleek and Larne. Larne can be dismissed very quickly since it functioned as a whiteware pottery for a very short period, and anything it produced at that time would be indistinguishable from the wares of the Clyde Pottery of Greenock whose owners worked Larne at that time. Beleek certainly made spongeware and sometimes marked it. But they seem to have made it in limited amounts and the body is very characteristic, seeming always to have a gray/green tinge. In the marked pieces the decoration often consists of two fairly simple motifs in contrasting colors. Most of the spongeware found in Ireland is of Scottish or English origin, most frequently the former. A huge trade was carried on between Ireland and western Scotland — with butter, eggs and bacon going one way and ironwork and ceramics going the other.

Towards the beginning of the twentieth century Adams of Stoke began production of a new line which they named **Titian Ware**. The body was of an ivory tint which agreed with the bright decoration. The decoration tends to be based on plant forms and is very exact and sharp-edged. It gives the impression of being sponge-printed but, in fact, seems to be entirely hand-painted. The term Titian Ware refers to the glaze; the body used is the ivory colored body so popular during that period since it complemented the strong colors used in Titian Ware and the wares of so many other potteries at that time. The mark is dated by Godden as being used from 1896 onwards and often contains the phrase "hand painted." However, the dates of registration of patterns for Titian Ware are usually somewhat later than this, being in the twentieth century. Titian Ware is now highly collected and prized for its brightness and high quality.

At the time of the First World War several British potteries began to produce patriotic spongeware. The main motifs were alternate crossed flags and crowns that varied in form from piece to piece. The color scheme was always red and blue. On straight-sided small bowls this decoration was on the interior rim and was accompanied by other decoration on the inside base. This was sometimes a patriotic motto in black sponge-printing, but was more often a complicated scene with soldiers or warships and a motto. The style of these scenes is so different from anything else seen on these bowls as to lead one to the conclusion that they were bought in. At a later date this whole scheme of decoration was adapted to the postwar world and was used for purposes other than the stirring of patriotic fervor.

By 1930 many potteries in Britain were experiencing a great deal of trouble staying open because of intense competition from potteries in Germany and Czechoslovakia, and many, particularly in Scotland, succumbed. At the same time tastes were changing and the days of spongeware were numbered. Certainly in the 1930s it completely disappeared from the scene. This was not the end of its story, however, since in the 1970s a number of studio potters began to experiment again with the manufacture of spongeware. Since the sponge roots required were not readily available they resorted to other carriers of color, one of them even using shock absorbers from motor cars. This experimentation agreed with a change in public taste. The wares were so successful that it is nowadays available from many commercial firms and can be found in any pottery bazaar. In recent years the technique has also been used in the production of goods for the tourist market in Cyprus.

One encounters great problems when wishing to see spongeware in a public collection. It is surprising how many of the world's great museums have little or none to show you in their reserve collections. The best collection known to me is in the Ulster Folk and Transport Museum. The Hunterian Museum of Glasgow University and the Highland Folk Museum at Kingussie also have small but useful collections. The Royal Museum of Scotland in Edinburgh has a collection, most of which is from Kirkcaldy. Other Scottish and English museums have small amounts. I have little information about Museums in Canada and the U.S.A. The International Museum of Ceramics in Faenza, Italy, has two or three pieces of Italian ware on exhibit.

When one looks at the spongeware available in different countries, a great deal of useful information can be obtained about the manufacturers' estimate of different markets. For instance, in Scotland, Canada and South Africa spongeware tends to be of the simplest kind and, particularly in Scotland, animals are a favorite motif in the pattern. Cows were particularly popular in Scotland. In Asia, on the other hand, the shapes, as one would expect, were styled to the market, but the whole style of the sponges changes. Although the transfer-printed wares were full of mythical animals, exotic fruit and other oriental motifs, the spongeware is abstract for the most part or shows highly stylized plant forms. It is a misfortune that Canadians and Americans are such indefatigable collectors since their scouring of the markets in so many countries and the workings of Canadian and American dealers have totally obscured what was sent out to North America in the first place. It can be surmised, however, that the principal supplier to the U.S.A. was the Staffordshire potteries and that other English and Scottish potteries played a minor part — a very different picture from that shown by Canada where the Scottish potteries played a major role. This may have been exaggerated though by the activity of dealers over the years. There is certainly a surprising lack of animal sponge prints in the Durrie collection and an inordinate number of child's tea sets. But both of these are perhaps due to his taste as a collector. In the same way, the spongeware exhibited by Finlayson in his book, *Portneuf Pottery,* almost certainly reflects the taste of collectors in Canada. The markets which are totally unknown still are the South American, the Australian and most of the African continent. Production in Eastern Europe is not well understood in the West although it is known to have been prolific.

Patterns in Spongeware Made by Several Potteries Over a Period of Time

1. **'Persian Rose'**—So named by Dilys Jenkins in her book *Llanelly Pottery* (listed above), never named by any pottery. There are three elements, two in brushstroke, one sponge-printed. Round the piece are a number of painted crimson flowers seen from the side, each with a green stem and leaves. These painted flowers are often in the U.S.A. referred to as the Adams Rose. It was certainly produced by Adams but also by many other potteries and there is no evidence that Adams originated it. The term is best kept to the single motif while the term Persian Rose is used for the typical pattern. Between each group there is a blue element, usually a number of blue, sponge-printed stars but occasionally a brushstroked bow. This is known to have been made in both England and Scotland over a long period. It was certainly being made by the Britannia Pottery in Glasgow in the 1930s and may still be in production in England.
2. **'Virginia'** — So named by Adams of Stoke; other potteries had other names for it, sometimes just a number, for instance to Petrus Regout and the Société Cêramique both it was No. 47. This is fairly similar to Persian Rose but the flower is trumpet shaped and has painted blue sepals. The sponge-printed element is violet and occurs amongst the green leaves rather than between motifs. Again it was widely made in at least three countries and over a long period.
3. **'Garden'**—A name of convenience never used by any pottery. The central element is a painted flower enclosed in a circle. From this spring three plants with sponge-printed flowers. Round the rim there is a sponge-printed, abstract motif which has painted foliage hanging from it. This is found widely on export wares destined for southeast Asia and was made in Holland, Scotland and England certainly and in a large number of color combinations. The element in this pattern comprising three sponged flowers with foliage has been referred to as Regout's Flowers, a name which is quite convenient so long as it is understood that many other potteries besides Regout used the motif, including Adams, Methven's Links Pottery and Bells' Glasgow Pottery.
4. **'Grecian'** — Already discussed. There is a central element of trophies (?) with a surrounding ring of leaflets. Then there are a number of groups with arrow-shaped leaves and finally a rim ringed with an abstract motif. Numerous pieces are known marked from Scottish and English potteries but there is a vast treasure of unmarked pieces that are impossible to attribute since variations are numberless. Curiously enough this pattern seems to be unknown as such to most writers on spongeware in the U.S.A.
5. The Robackers' have given many names to pieces but when looked at closely one usually finds that the name has been given to a single motif or to a type of motif. The most useful is perhaps **'Bullseye'** which is used for any pattern which consists of a number of concentric lines with bands of sponge-printing between.

Spongeware

Animals

The classification of spongeware by subject matter or by techniques used, very rarely gives a consistent group of pieces but pieces with mammals as subjects seem to be the exception. This group shows a remarkable consistency and most of them must be attributed to Scottish potteries. This does not include, of course, birds or other animals whose use seems to be more widespread. Indeed, it may be that a few of the mammal pieces are of English origin but the evidence would be all to the contrary.

The strongest evidence for a Scottish origin is the distribution. The greatest concentration of pots with mammal motifs is still in Scotland, Ireland and Canada, in all of which Scotland was the main source of supply. This is true in spite of the fierce collecting activity in the U.S.A. over the years. Of the few pieces which can be given a definite pottery of origin that pottery is Scottish.

Animals found on spongeware include cows, deer, reindeer, dogs, cats, horses, tigers, lizards, pigs, and elephants. The most commonly found of these, curiously, are cows and deer (including reindeer).

Birds and butterflies are a different matter altogether. Butterfly pieces were made by Clyde Pottery in Greenock, by Llanelly Pottery in Llanelli and by various French potteries, as well, no doubt, as by many others. Birds as motifs seem to have been used universally, both those approximating to real birds and creatures of fantasy. Cockerels were understandably popular in France but hand-painted cockerel plates became a standard product of Llanelly Pottery too and achieved great local fame. The bat-tailed bird is, on sherd evidence, usually attributed to Bo'ness Pottery.

3. Plate with molded border - c. 6.75" (17 cm). Sponge printed with a black cat and molded border covered in yellow. **No mark.** Possibly Scottish. £200, $400.

4. Mug. c. 4" high (10.25 cm). Sponge printed with a cow standing in grass with foliage. At least one complex sponge with brown and two greens; the second sponge has only the darker green and there is a band of sponge printing in a darker brown round the rim. **No mark.** Probably Scottish. Collection: Hunterian Museum, University of Glasgow. £180, $360.

Top left: 5. Mug. c. 4″ high (10.25 cm). Sponge printed in brown with a "cow on fibre." The very irregular sponging in slightly different arrangements of cow, fibre and plant give the piece a great deal of charm. **No mark.** Almost certainly Scottish. £180, $360.

Center: 7. Bowl. c. 5″ diameter (12.7 cm). Sponge printed with motifs similar to those in 5. **No mark.** Probably Scottish. £170, $340.

Bottom left: 8. Mug. c. 4″ high (10.25 cm). Sponge printed in sepia with cows in a floral scene. **No mark.** Possibly Scottish. Collection: Ulster Folk and Transport Museum, NMGNI. £180, $360.

Top right: 6. Bowl. c. 5″ (12.7 cm) in diameter. Sponge printed with very similar motifs to 5. **No mark.** Almost certainly Scottish. Highland Folk Museum, Kingussie, Highland Council. £170, $340.

Bottom right: 9. Bowl. c. 5″ diam. (12.7 cm). Sponge printed with "cows on fibre" in indigo. **No mark.** Very similar to 5 and probably Scottish. Collection: Ulster Folk and Transport Museum, NMGNI. £170, $340.

10. Mug. c. 4" high (10.25 cm). Sponge printed in brown with cows in a landscape with gate, similar to 5 etc. above. **No mark.** Probably Scottish. Collection: Ulster Folk and Transport Museum, NMGNI. £180, $360.

11. Mug. c. 4" high (10.25 cm). Sponge printed in brown with "cows on fibre," very similar to 5 etc. **No mark.** Probably Scottish. Collection: Ulster Folk and Transport Museum, NMGNI. £180, $360.

12. Mug. c. 4" high (10.25 cm). Sponge printed in sepia with cows on a fibrous ground with a simple lined rim. This differs in several respects from the previous group, certainly enough for us to speculate on whether it originated in another pottery. Nevertheless, in spite of the lack of a mark, it seems reasonable to label it "probably Scottish." Collection: Ulster Folk and Transport Museum, NMGNI. £180, $360.

13. & 14. Mug. c. 4" high (10.25 cm). Sponge printed in sepia with "cows on grass" and stylized leafy rim band. **No mark** but this one can be definitely assigned to the Bridgeness Pottery of C. W. McNay in Bo'ness on the evidence of other pieces in known McNay shapes. Collection: Hunterian Museum, University of Glasgow. £180, $360.

16. Sherd very similar to 15, found in Bo'ness.

15. Mug. c. 4" high (10.25 cm). Sponge printed in sepia with cows on a ground very similar to 12 and possibly from the same pottery. Simple lined rim. **No mark.** £180, $360.

17. Bowl. c. 10" (25.4 cm). Blue lining with alternating light green and red floral motifs at the everted rim. Centrally there is a very complex sponge print in sepia, dark green and red of a cow in a rudimentary landscape. **No mark.** Probably Scottish. £250, $500.

18. Pitcher. c. 8" high (20.5 cm). Printed in sepia with "cow in grass" in a central band and floral motifs at rim and base. **No mark.** The jug shape is known to have been made at the Bridgeness Pottery of C. W. McNay c. 1900. **See no. 13**. £250, $500.

19. Bowl. c. 5" (12.7 cm). Printed in sepia with cows on a textured ground. **No mark.** Probably Scottish. £170, $340.

20. Bowl. c. 5" (12.7 cm). Printed in blue with "cows on grass" and a rim motif (see no. 13). Almost certainly Bridgeness Pottery, c. 1900. £180, $360.

21. Detail from plate. Central motif is a cow in a landscape. The sponge is complex using crimson and green. The plate had a red floral sponged border between two green lines.

22. Bowl. c. 5" (12.7 cm). Border motifs in sepia of holly leaves and berries. Central band of complex sponges in black and green of a dog. **No mark.** This specimen was found in Ireland but most dog pieces have been reported from Scotland. £190, $380.

23. Pitcher. c. 8" (20.5 cm). Bands of black motif at rim and base. There is a central very complex sponge in brown, red, green, yellow and blue of a stag in a landscape. **No mark.** The shape of this jug would warrant an attribution to the Britannia Pottery of Robert Cochran and a date in the 1870s but one specimen is known with a T molded on the base which has given rise to much speculation.

24. Cream jug. Sponge printed in sepia with a border of solid color with entwined ropes in negative and pendants as well as a stag in a landscape as the main motif on each side. The border is clobbered with amber lustre and the landscape in red, green and yellow. **No mark** but the use of amber lustre and the style of the piece would suggest a Scottish origin, as well as the fact that its earliest known find spot is in Scotland. Collection: Hunterian Museum, University of Glasgow. £130, $260.

25. Bowl. c. 5" (12.7 cm) diam. The rim has a band of pink floral motifs. The main body has a sponge printed band of reindeer on grass in brown and green. **No mark.** Probably Scottish. £250, $500.

26. Bowl. c. 9.5" (24.1 cm). Very similar to no. 25. Bands of pink motifs at rim and base and central group of reindeer in brown and dark green. **No mark.** Probably Scottish. £90, $180.

27. Mug. 3.75" (9.5 cm) in height and width. The top band is red. Three reindeer in brown and green from a multicolored sponge. Finlayson called this a moose, which seems unlikely in view of its Scottish origin. £100, $200.

28. Plate. 6.25" (15.9 cm). Molded border and red rim line. A central, complex, multicolored sponge print with deer in brown, green, red and yellow. £150, $300.

29. Pitcher. c. 8″ high (20.32 cm). Rim and base have band of brown motif covered in amber lustre. Centrally, each side has a sponge print of a deer in a landscape in brown with crimson, yellow and green. **No mark.** Probably Scottish. £100, $200.

30. Mug. A simple crimson line at the edge of the rim and a print of a stag in green and sepia complete the simple decoration of this mug. **No mark.** £150, $300.

Center left and above: 31 and 32. Punch bowl printed in brown with a stag in a landscape. This is clobbered in red and green. The rim and base on the interior and exterior have a band of a wheel-like motif which connects this piece very strongly with 23. **No mark.** £200, $400, £100, $200.

33. Plate with molded wheat. 8.875″ (22.4 cm). Red lines over the wheat and a border of red squirrels. The inner circle is green. **No mark.** £250, $500.

34. Mug. c. 4" (10.2 cm). Printed in sepia with a band of leaf motifs at the rim and a central scene which is virtually the Belleek Pottery mark which almost certainly gives us the origin of the piece. Collection: Ulster Folk and Transport Museum, NMGNI. £200, $400.

35. Sherd. Sponge printed in purple with a leafy rim motif and centrally a jockey on horseback. This sherd and a fragment of a similar one in blue were found on a sherd dump in northern Glasgow. Unfortunately the dump was not exclusive to one pottery but had identifiable transfer-printed sherds from both Bells' and Britannia, one of whom must have been responsible for this pattern. No complete piece has ever been recorded.

36. Plate. c. 8" (20.3 cm). Flow blue and sponge printed throughout with a central elephant. **No mark.** Perhaps Scottish. A very similar plate has been recorded in Myanmar (Burma). £250, $500.

Center right: 37. Plate. c. 5" (12.7 cm). Crimson lines enclose a band of blue motifs. Centrally is a painted cockerel in several colors. This type of plate is known to have been made at Llanelly Pottery in Llanelli in Wales and painted by Sarah Roberts. **No mark.** £150, $300.

38. Plate. 9.75" (24.7cm). All in pale blue with cockerels and flowers. **No mark.** £80, $160.

39. Plate. 9.75" (24.7 cm). Red lines and blue sponged border. The center shows a cockerel in red, blue and other colors. **No mark** but certainly from Llanelly Pottery in Llanelli, Wales, and painted by Sarah Roberts. £150, $300.

40. Soup plate. 9" (22.9 cm). A cockerel painted in red, green and yellow on a green sponged ground. Five blue stencilled units on the flange. **No mark.** £60, $120.

41. Lidded dish. c. 3" high. (7.2 cm). A brown geometric motif in a band at the rim of both lid and bowl and centrally a rather crude print of a cockerel in brown clobbered in brown, yellow and green. **No mark.** Origin unknown. £100, $200.

42. Molded bowl. c. 5.5" diam. (14 cm). Medallions on lid and body are filled with cockerels printed in red, yellow and green (perhaps stencilled). These sit on grass printed in two shades of green and resting on crimson lines. **No mark.** Probably Scottish. £100, $200.

43. Pudding plate. c. 5″ (12.7 cm). Lined in green and printed in green and brown with a cockerel on grass surmounted by the phrase GUID MORNIN'. **No mark** but the phrase marks the piece as almost certainly of Scottish origin and certainly meant for the Scottish market. £180, $360.

44. Mug. c. 3.5″ (8.9 cm). A printed brown cockerel on each side is clobbered in red, blue, yellow and green. The treatment of the ground is reminiscent of no. 41. **No mark.** Origin unknown. £80, $160.

45. Mug. Blue line at rim and a band of green grass on which a cockerel stands in a complex print of black, blue and red. **No mark.** £120, $240.

46. Bowl. 6.625″ (16.8 cm) x 2.25″ (5.7 cm). Green lines and swags with brown shamrocks and a cockerel which stands on a green patch. The lettering is black with shamrocks and the motto indicates an aim for the Irish market but these bowls are usually of Scottish or Welsh origin. The Scottish examples are usually attributed to the Links Pottery of Kirkcaldy, the Welsh ones to Llanelly Pottery. **No mark.** £150, $300.

47. Bowl. c. 5.5″ diam. (14 cm). A crimson line is the only rim decoration. A complex sponge shows a red-breasted bird in a wreath. The colors are crimson, black and green. There is an identical motif on the interior of the bowl. Bowls with this pattern have been found in Glasgow, Belfast and the U.S.A. The Irish specimen had a hole through the center of the interior bird as if for nailing to a wall. There is **no mark** but the origin is certainly Scottish. Collection: Hunterian Museum, University of Glasgow. £100, $200.

48. Bowl. 6.75 x 3.125″ (17.1 x 7.9 cm). A red line with five repeats of the black robin with a red breast in a green wreath in a composite, three-color print. A sixth robin is inside the bowl. Bought in Canada but others which are identical except for size have been found in Glasgow and Belfast. Glasgow is almost certainly the place of origin. One specimen had a hole bored through the center of the base as if for hanging on a wall. **No mark.** £150, $300.

49. Another specimen of the same pattern. £150, $300.

50. Mug. 4.375″ (1.1 cm). An upper band of motifs in brown and a lower in blue. The birds are multi-color prints in blue/green, green and red. **No mark.** £90, $180.

51. Plate. c. 8.5" (21.5 cm). Blue lines enclose a crimson band of motifs of rope with elaborate crosses between the strands. The center has a large sponge print of a peacock in green, blue and brown. **No mark.** A similar plate has been recorded with a sponge printed anchor and rope as a backstamp but this is so far no help in attributing the plates. £180, $360.

52. Plate. 6.375" (16.2 cm). A molded border. A multicolored peacock and branches using one or more complex sponges. Such plates are found from time to time in Britain, usually unmarked but sometimes with an unattributable black sponge printed anchor. A skilled and relatively expensive item. £150, $300.

53. Plate. 9.75" (24.7 cm). All in pale blue. Three peacocks and flowers. **No mark.** £90, $180.

54. Mug. c. 4" high (10.2 cm). There is a thick crimson line at the rim. The central motif is "the bat-tailed bird" in a complex sponge with crimson, green and blue. This motif is attributed to Bo'ness Pottery on the strength of sherds found in the area but still unpublished. Collection: Hunterian Museum, University of Glasgow. £130, $260.

55. Bowl. c. 9" diam (22.9 cm). A red rim line surmounts a repeated complex motif of a fantasy bird in crimson, green and brown. There is a resemblance to the bat-tailed bird **in illustration no. 54** but not strong enough for an attribution to the same pottery. Bowls of this type are usually attributed to the Links Pottery of Kirkcaldy, but this is only a traditional attribution. **No mark.** £100, $200.

56. Bowl with same dimensions as no. 55. This time the rim has a band of brown motifs and the fantasy bird is in green, crimson and yellow. Otherwise the two bowls are very similar. £130, $260.

57. Bowl. All sponge printing is in brown. The rim has elaborate decoration with two rows of checks and a triangular hanging motif below. The central motif is a bird perched on a twig. **No mark.** £90, $180.

58. and 59. Punch bowl. The abstract rim motif and the principal motif inside and out are all in brown but there is clobbering in red, yellow and green and large crimson blossoms. **No mark.** £200, $400.

60. Bowl. c. 6.5″ (16.5 cm). A crimson rim line and a complex sponge in crimson, black and green make up the whole decoration of this piece. **No mark.** £150, $300.

61. Mug. c. 4.5″ (11.1 cm). A rather unusual crimson floral or fruit motif decorates the rim. The main body has a complex sponge in green, crimson and blue of two birds perched on a twig. **No mark.** £130, $260.

62. Mug. c. 4.5″ (11.1 cm). A pink target motif makes a band round the rim while each side has a complex sponge in green, yellow and crimson of two birds perched on a twig with fruit. **No mark.** £90, $180.

63. Bowl. c. 3.5″ (8.9 cm). Rather crude decoration. The rim has a series of arches with rosettes in pink and below this are green flying birds, probably meant for thrushes. **No mark.** Collection: Kingussie, The Highland Folk Museum, Highland Council. £100, $200.

65. Bowl. c. 10″ (25.4 cm). A crimson rim line and two rows of a complex, repeating motif of a bird and flowers in brown, red and green. **No mark.** £100, $200.

64. Bowl. c. 8″ (20.3 cm). Beneath a crimson rim line is a band of black floral motifs. The main decoration is a complex, repeating sponge of a bird on a bough in pink, green and brown. **No mark.** £100, $200.

66. Bowl. A rim band of a brown motif of some complexity. The main body has a repeating motif of a bird with flowers in brown and pink. **No mark.** £90, $180.

67. Plate. The scrolled rim has a band of brown motifs which seem to be the only sponged elements. The center has a largely painted scene of a bird on a bough in green, brown, blue and black. **No mark.** This is a rather sophisticated piece which looks late and perhaps Continental. Collection: Ulster Folk and Transport Museum, NMGNI. £80, $160.

68. Plate. A violet rim motif surmounts three flying birds in complex sponges of green, blue and black also on the rim. Beneath each bird, on the body of the plate is a pair of light green leaves. **No mark.** This plate is unusual both in colouring and in the arrangement of the sponges. £40, $80.

69. and 70. Plate and detail. The rim motif is brown forming a band round the edge. In the well of the plate are four birds in brown, perched on pink twigs. **No mark.** £110, $220.

71. and 72. Plate and detail. c. 9" (22.9 cm). Decorated in brown with a complicated floral border and a floral center with birds. The birds are perhaps meant as peacocks. **No mark.** £100, $200.

73. Detail of a plate printed in brown with floral motifs and flying birds. **No mark.** £100, $200.

74. Mug. 4″ x 4″ (10.1 cm). All in brown. Three repeats of two birds on a branch. The mug is almost certainly Scottish. The rim motif is similar to some found on butterfly bowls from Clyde Pottery, Greenock. £80, $160.

75. Soup plate. 9.5″ (24.1 cm). A blue line, 15 blue swans, 6 green bows and 6 dark blue geometric forms. **No mark.** £130, $260.

76. Mug. 3.375″ (8.6 cm). Twelve birds in brown and red in green foliage. Complex, multicolored sponges. **No mark.** £100, $200.

77. Pitcher. 6″ high (15.2 cm). A blue rim line and a band of yellow sponging. The main body is occupied by a painted bird on a bough in red, green, yellow, blue and brown. **Mark: AULD HEATHER WARE**, from the Links Pottery, Kirkcaldy. **See Mark no. 114A.** £180, $360.

78. Bowl. 8.875 x 1.625" (22.4 x 4.1 cm). A blue, sponge printed border. The bird is a black outline with brown, pink and blue plumage. The branches are black and the foliage has been dabbed in gray/green. **No mark.** £70, $140.

79. Bowl. 8.75 x 1.5" (22 x 3.8 cm). Black lines enclose a sponge printed border. The center has a bird on a bough painted in yellow, brown and black with green, sponge printed foliage. **Mark: impressed AMBERG**. German, late 19th century. £110, $220.

See *Zuhlsdorff,* p. 393 where Adolph Amberg is recorded as a modeler in Germany from 1878 to 1913. Also see Mark 2.63, p. 124

80. Bowl. c. 6" (15.2 cm). All in purple. A band of Greek Key at the rim and below a sponged representation of a bird perched on a twig. **No mark.** £80, $160.

81. Mug. The rim has a band of blue motifs while the center has a crude but complex, repeating motif of a butterfly in red, brown and green. **No mark.** £110, $220.

82. Soup plate. 9.75" diam. (25 cm). Brown lines enclose a band of blue flower motifs on the rim. The well is covered with an elaborate stencil in crimson, green, blue and brown of a butterfly amongst flowers. **Mark: DIGOUIN & SARREGUEMINES** round a crowned shield with various technical marks both impressed and stamped. **Also see Mark 337 and KAD No. C47**. £120, $240.

83. Bowl c. 5" diam. (12.7 cm). The rim has a crimson line and the bottom a continuous band of green grass. Between is a complex but fairly crude sponge of a butterfly in crimson, green and yellow. **No mark.** £90, $180.

84. Cup and saucer. Red butterflies. **No mark.** £50, $100.

85. Soup plate. 10.875" (27.6 cm). Painted flowers in red and blue with green foliage and a blue rim line. There are four blue, sponge printed butterflies. **No mark.** £150, $300.

86. Punch bowl. 10″ x 5.75″ (25.4 x 14.6 cm). A brown, sponged band of butterflies and Prince of Wales feathers and the sponged border are painted with amber lustre. The red and green foliage is painted. This was bought in Canada and was certainly made at Clyde Pottery, Greenock, Scotland, where sherds of the pattern were found in an excavation on the site of the Pottery. Bowls of a smaller size without the feathers but with the butterflies are still quite commonly found in western Scotland. **No mark.** £250, $500.

87. Invalid spit pot. Over a pale pink wash the sponge printing is all in gray. A floral border is above butterfly motifs. **No mark.** £100, $200.

88. Rice dish. Crimson lines enclose groups of crimson dots between oval motifs in black, one of which is repeated in the center. Beneath the crimson lines are eight black motifs of a lizard (or a monkey?) on a twig. Perhaps originally meant for export. **No mark.** Collection: Kingussie, Highland Folk Museum, Highland Council. £250, $500.

89. Bowl. 6.75″ diam (17.5 cm). Two blue lines enclose a very complicated series of decorations. Four panels show a black print of a monkey climbing a stick against a background of painted yellow lines and enclosed by painted brown lines. This alternates with a larger panel divided into four by two crimson lines, each quarter having a sponge printed leafy motif in green. The interior has a painted blue line. **The only mark is a painted blue dash**. Wherever this bowl was made, it seems likely that its intended destination was West Africa. £300, $600.

90. Pudding plate with molded rim. The rim is painted blue and the well contains a stencilled bird in black. There is no sponge printing here but the plate is included because of its similarity to illustration no. 3. £40, $80.

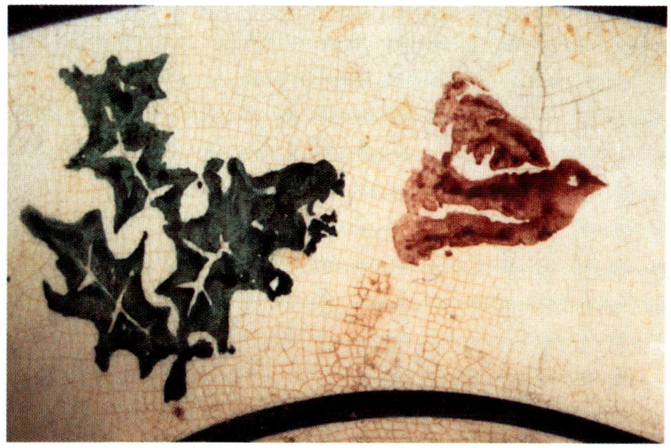

91. Detail of green-banded bowl showing bird in flight. £200, $400.

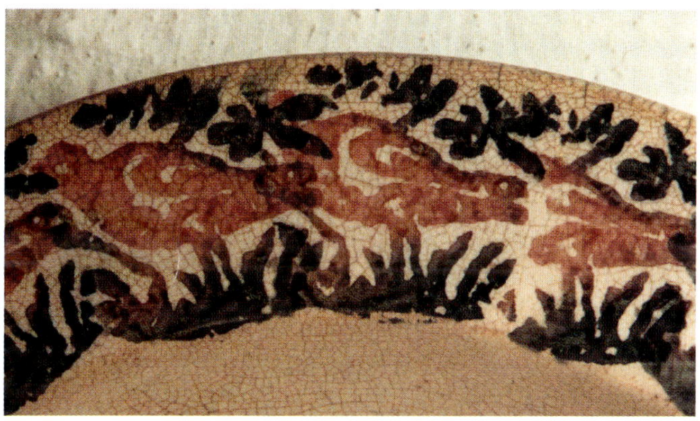

92. Detail of plate rim showing band of birds on grass in pink and green. **No mark.** £170, $340.

93. Plate. c. 8″ (20.3 cm). Rim band of brown chain motif, then three rows of blue anchors and a central complex sponge of a sailing boat in yellow and green. **No mark.** £250, $500.

94. Bowl. 9.25 x 2″ (23.5 x 5.1 cm). The fish border and the inner chain are sponge printed in dark olive. The lines are light blue. The central ship seems to be sponge printed in black. **No mark.** £200, $400.

95. Bowl. 4.875" (12.4 cm). The top line is black, the bottom blue. Between are pale blue fish and seaweed motifs. Glaze faults. **No mark.** £110, $220.

Scotland

There are distinct difficulties in attributing pieces here since so many potteries did not mark their spongeware. Scottish potteries seem to have been more reluctant than most to mark their spongewares. Methven's Links Pottery is the big exception; their everyday spongeware was, perhaps, not marked any more than anyone else's but they had three categories, made for special destinations which were always marked. Airlie Ware was made for a dealer in Kirriemuir; Nisbet Ware for another in Edinburgh and Auld Heather Ware was made specifically for the market in the U.S.A., though one lot was dumped on the home market. All three wares were identical and all date from the latest period in the Pottery's life. It needs to be emphasized, though, that all Scottish whiteware potteries made spongeware and continued to make it well into the twentieth century.

The "green-banded bowls" also present a slight problem. These are straight-sided bowls decorated in the interior with green painted bands, between which is a row of sponge printed motifs. The floor of the bowl is often decorated with a couthy motto in black, sometimes sponged, sometimes impressed and printed both. This may or may not be accompanied by a sponged motif. The vast majority of these bowls are certainly Scots but there are a few which were equally certainly made at the Llanelly Pottery. The most favored candidate for the source in Scotland in the Links Pottery but this, although likely, is by no means proved. One is shown here destined for the Irish market and here several other Scottish potteries had a bigger stake than Links.

Closely connected with these are the "patriotic" wares, showing flags, wartime scenes and mottoes. The flags, quite often look vaguely like the Union Jack and the Stars and Stripes but this must not be taken to indicate an export product since the vast majority of these pieces are found in Scotland or England. Most are certainly Scottish in origin but some may well be English since, by the time of the First World War, there were few Scottish potteries capable of making them. The scenes on the interior floor of the bowls are certainly bought in, since the precision of the engraving is at complete odds with the transfer products of the same period.

As well as this, of course, Methven, Bell and Cochran all made wares for the Asian market which were much more scrupulously marked, but these are totally different from everyday spongeware and are treated here in a different category.

So far sherds of an early type have been found in excavation on the sites of Bells' and Bo'ness Pottery but it would be unwise to attribute the origin of spongeware to either of these since they are almost the only large whiteware potteries to have been subject to excavation. Nevertheless the finding of such early-looking wares must contribute to the idea that spongeware originated in Scotland. The section starts with two typologically early, unmarked pieces of pottery which were both found some time ago in Scotland and are assumed to have originated there since they were found before collecting became general.

96. and 97. Pie dish. c. 5" (12.7 cm). Printed overall inside and out with a single motif made from a loosely textured sponge. **No mark.** £180, $360.

98. Bowl. c. 11" (27.9 cm). Printed on the outside with two motifs in three rows in blue throughout. The sponges bear no relationship to external objects as is most common with early spongeware. The bowl shows evidence of several thumb print smears but was marketed nonetheless. **No mark.** £300, $600.

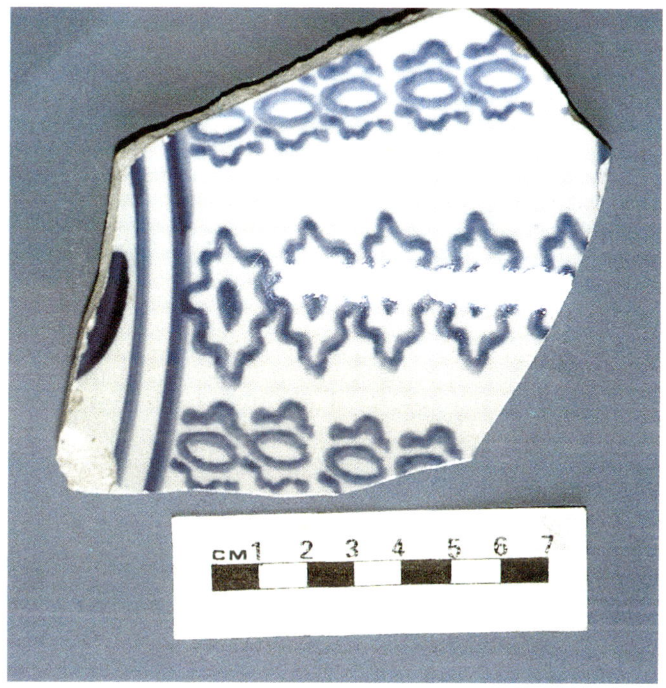

99. Sherd printed in blue and lined in the same color. This was found in the debris after the site of Bells' Pottery had been dug and then partly built over. **No mark.** It is dateable to shortly before 1860.

100. Sherds found on the site of Bells' Pottery after the dig and building operations. Again the date is before 1860. All of the sherds shown in no. 99 and no. 100 are relatively undeveloped; the patterns are unrelated to real objects and the cutting of the sponges is less assured than it later became.

101. Plate. c. 8" (20.3 cm). The pattern is **GRECIAN** printed in its most typical color - gray. Bells' version is readily recognizable by the feathery fronds at the top and by the drawing of the right-hand side. **Mark: printed B in a bell**. Date: c. 1880. Also see KAD B222. £20, $40.

102. Bowl. c. 4" (10.2 cm). "Scottish flow blue." This one bears the **Bells' mark of a St. Andrew's Saltire and an impressed bell. See KAD B220**. £50, $100.

103. Bowl with everted rim. c. 9" (22.9 cm). "Scottish flow blue." In this case the interior is covered in brushstoke but the outer surface is sponge printed in a somewhat indeterminate motif. **Bells' saltire mark.** £90, $180.

104. Plate. c. 8" (20.3 cm). Bells' version of **PERSIAN ROSE**. There is no sponge printing involved here but it is included to show what some potteries made of the universal pattern. **Mark: an impressed B in a bell.** Date: c. 1890. See KAD B222. £150, $300.

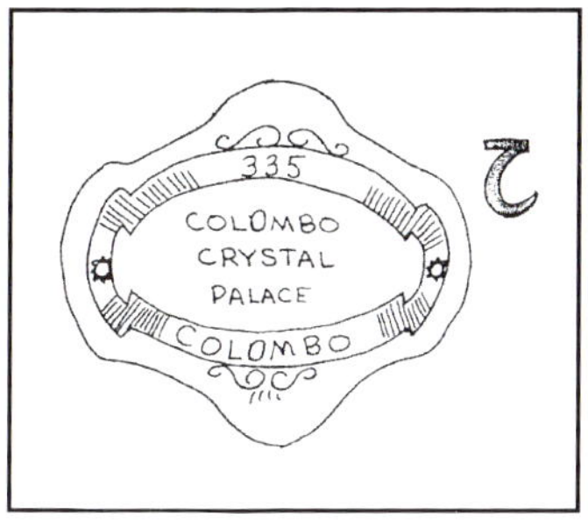

105A

105. Rice dish. 8.25 x 1.75" (20.9 x 4.4 cm). The rim line and four flowers are red, the foliage green and the sponge printed flowers blue. Mark: three indecipherable initials above **COLUMBO CRYSTAL PALACE** with **COLUMBO** below. This backstamp has been reported from the Glasgow Pottery of J. & M.P. Bell & CO. but the pattern was also made for export by a number of potteries in three countries. **See mark no. 105A.** £100, $200.

106. Molded sherd found on the site of Bo'ness Pottery during building operations. It shows signs of sponge printing in blue and is shown here with an unmarked bowl with similar moldings, sponge printed round the rim in blue. **No mark.** £40, $80.

107. Plate 9. 625" (24.4 cm). Sepia decorated throughout. Similar plates in Britain are often attributed to W. McNay' s Bridgeness Pottery, Bo'ness. The central scene is thought to be bat-printed or rubber-stamped. **No mark.** £80, $160.

108. and **mark 108A**. Mug. c. 4" (10.2 cm). Band of blue double diamond motifs round the rim. The main body has flowers printed in a single sponge with crimson and green. £90, $180.

110. Mug. c. 4" (10.2 cm). Lines in black, red, yellow and green enclose a band of red motifs. From the green line depend "flares" in crimson and yellow and groups of flowers in blue and green. This is a very common pattern used by the Links Pottery on their better spongewares. **Mark: AIRLIE WARE stamped in black.** £80, $160.

111. Vase. c. 8" (20.3 cm). This is the Links Pottery's version of **PERSIAN ROSE** with an extra little floral motif on the neck of the vase and a Wemyss Ware type fringe at the rim. **Mark: AIRLIE WARE, stamped in black.** £150, $300.

112. Two jam pots. Left-hand has **PERSIAN ROSE**; the right-hand has a three flower pattern in blue, yellow and green, found very often on Methven's wares. It is nevertheless not made by Methven. It is marked **LOMOND WARE**, known to have been decorated by Frank Young outwith the Links Pottery. The right-hand pot is **AIRLIE WARE** by Methven. £60, $120 & £70, $140.

113. Pitcher. c. 5" (12.7 cm). The very complicated pattern with blue lining and at least four sponges in three different colors is found very commonly on the wares of the Links Pottery. This one is **unmarked.** £80, $160.

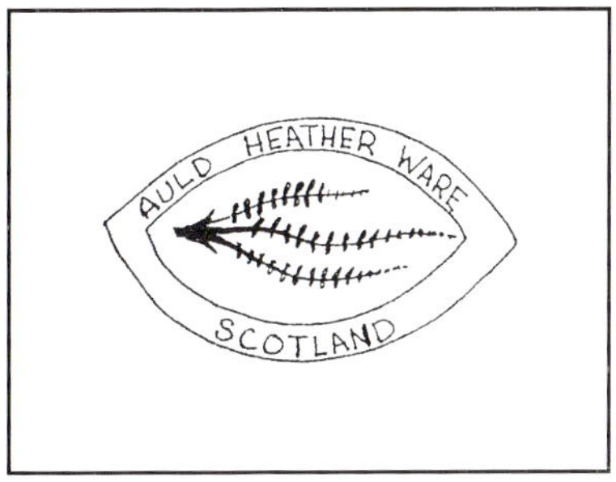

114A

114. Plate. 8.875" (22.4 cm). Black and yellow bands, large yellow flowers, green foliage and sponged blue flowers with yellow centers. **Mark: AULD HEATHER WARE SCOTLAND** for the Links Pottery, Kirkcaldy. **See Mark no. 114A.** £80, $160.

116. Butter dish in three parts (the third part is an interior insert not shown in the photograph). 7.5" (19.1 cm) square. A sponge printed blue band between yellow lines. Above are blue sponged flowers with green foliage and red flares. **See Mark no. 114A**. £120, $240.

115. Vegetable dish with lid. 9.75 x 8.5 x 5.5" (24.7 x 21.6 x 14 cm). An animal finial. A red rim line and blue sponge printed border on the dish and cover. The cover also has red flowers with yellow centers, red buds and foliage in two greens and blue. **Mark: AULD HEATHER WARE SCOTLAND - See Mark no. 114A.** £120, $240.

117. Sugar basin. 4" (10.2 cm). The colors and patterns are the same as in no. 116. **See Mark no. 114A.** £110, $220.

118. The **AULD HEATHER WARE** mark. Made for the American market, it used yellow more liberally than other potteries. Commonly also found in Scotland. **See Mark no. 114A**.

119. Serving dish. 9.25 x 7 x 2″ (23.5 x 17.8 x 5.1 cm). Blue sponge printed border with red line. Otherwise the usual colors. **See Mark no. 114A.** £100, $200.

120. Sauce boat and underdish. Blue lines enclose black sponged motifs on a brown dabbed ground. Flares in red and green hang from this. The bottom line gives rise to blue sponged flowers with green painted foliage. **See Mark no. 114A**. £90, $180.

121. and 122. Charger. 13″ (33 cm) and plate 7″ (17.8 cm). A red sponge printed band between blue lines. Four red and yellow painted flares with clusters of blue sponged flowers and green foliage. **See Mark no. 114A**. £150, $300 and £120, $240.

123. Platter or ashet. 5.5 x 4.5" (14 x 11,4 cm). A border of black sponge printed motifs over red dabbing between blue lines. **See Mark no. 114A**. £100, $200.

124. Plate 7.625" (19.4 cm). Red lines with pendant blue leaves, red flowers, green foliage, all sponge printed. **See Mark no. 114A**. £110, $220.

125. Plate. 8" (20.3 cm). Red lines enclose a band of black, sponge printed motifs over green dabbing. The center has painted flowers in red, yellow and two shades of green. **See Mark no. 114A**. £90, $180.

Fife Pottery also made spongeware, though marked specimens have not yet been found. They are known, however, to have made wares for Norman Franks, a London dealer and these pieces bear his mark: **See Mark No's. 126A and 128A.**

127. Plate. 8.5" (21.6 cm). **VIRGINIA**. **See Mark no. 128A**. £50, $100.

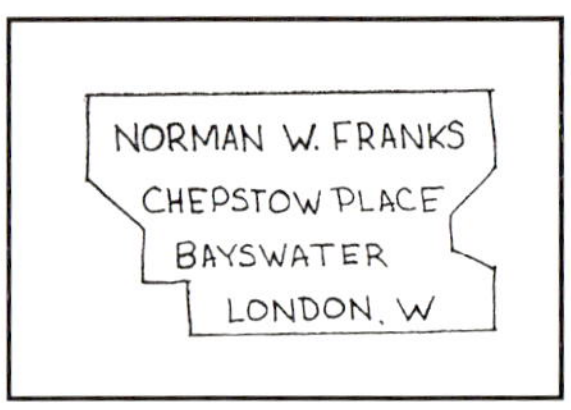

126. Rice dish. 10.25 x 2.25" (26 x 5.7 cm). **VIRGINIA** with red lines. **See Mark no. 128A**. £60, $120.

126A

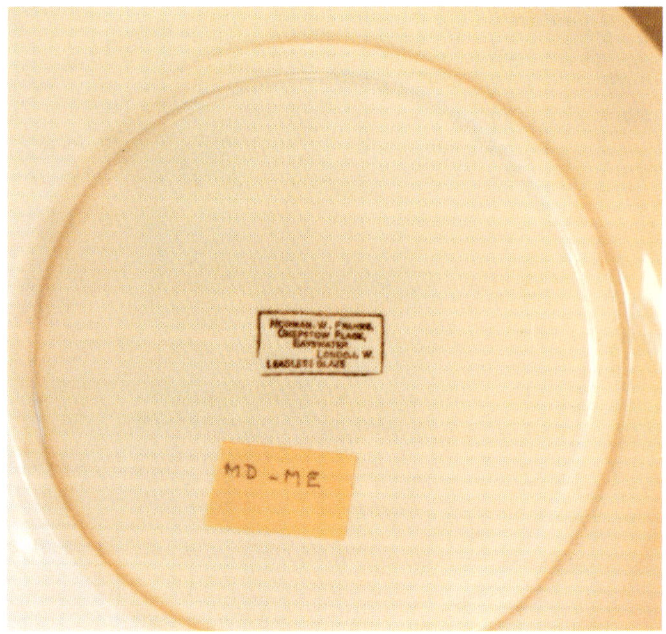

128. Mark for **NORMAN W. FRANKS CHEPSTOW PLACE BAYSWATER LONDON W. LEADLESS GLAZE**. This was a dealer who undoubtedly bought pieces in the **VIRGINIA** pattern from the Fife Pottery of Robert Heron in Kirkcaldy, since they have been identified through characteristic shapes. So this seems a likely origin for nos. 126 and 127. **See Mark No. 128A.**

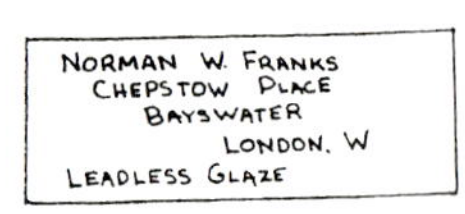

128A

129. Sugar basin with lid. 5.5" high (14 cm). Red rim lines and large flowers, small yellow flowers and green foliage. Blue sponged fans. Mark: the **NORMAN FRANKS mark as in 126A.** £110, $220.

130. Lidless jam pot with **VIRGINIA** bearing the **NORMAN FRANKS mark as before**. £50, $100.

131. Bowl. 9" (23 cm). Painted red "asters" are joined by a thin black line which has painted green and yellow foliage and sponge printed blue fans. **Norman Franks mark as before**. £90, $180.

132. Slop jar (These are sometimes referred to as bread bins). 14.75" (37.5 cm). Red lines and large red flowers next to paired blue flowers, alternating with green leaves. The top band on the jar is blue. The handles on this piece correspond closely to handles on known Fife Pottery pieces. **No mark.** £300, $600.

133. and 134. Pitcher. c. 5" (12.7 cm). Bearing the Norman Franks mark and of a definite Fife Pottery shape. **VIRGINIA** pattern. Part of the Britannia metal lid has been lost. £40, $80.

135. Sherds. Found on the site of the Victoria Pottery, Pollokshaws, Glasgow, after building work had taken place on it.

140. Plate. c. 9″ (22.9 cm). **PERSIAN ROSE** with a blue sponge print. **Mark: B.P. CO. Ltd**. for the Britannia Pottery, St. Rollox, Glasgow. c. 1930. **See KAD B363**. £90, $180.

Top left: 136. Punch bowl - interior showing sepia sponge print with amber lustre and green lining. **No mark.** This is a known shape from Victoria Pottery and this type of decoration is also found quite often. Collection: Hunterian Museum, University of Glasgow. £190, $380.

Top right: 137. Pitcher. c. 8″ (20.3 cm). Decorated entirely in gray. A known pitcher shape from Victoria Pottery. **No mark.** c. 1878. Collection: Hunterian Museum, University of Glasgow. £120, $240.

Center left: 138. Punch bowl. Same shape as 136. **GRECIAN** in the usual gray. Victoria Pottery. **No mark.** c. 1878. £100, $200.

Center right: 139. Wall plaque. 10″ diam (25.4 cm). Transfer printed and clobbered and dabbed with blue. **Mark: D.L. & CO. (David Lockhart & CO.) LIFE-BUOY. See KAD B1462.** £100, $200.

141A

141. Plate. 6.375" (16.2 cm). Two bands of blue sponge printed motifs with flowers in red, yellow and blue. Green foliage. **Mark: SCOTCH IVORY, B. P. CO. Ltd., MADE IN SCOTLAND**. The pattern name is **WILD FLOWER. See Mark 141A.** £130, $260.

142. Platter or ashet. 11.625 x 9.5" (29.5 x 24.1 cm). The border and the central oblong are sponged in blue/green. The sponged flowers are red with dark green centers. The foliage is light green with yellow dots. **Mark: SCOTCH IVORY, B. P. CO. Ltd., MADE IN SCOTLAND**. £130, $260.s

143. Cream jug and saucer. 5.5" (14 cm), high and 5.3" (13.5 cm) diam. respectively. Brown sponge printing with overlying amber luster. The floral unit which is probably sponge printed is clobbered in green and pink. Many similar pieces are known from the Clyde Pottery in Greenock. £85, $170.

144. Bowl. 9.875" (16.75 cm). "Scottish flow blue." The outer surface has a sponge printed leaf motif which is repeated on the interior with some brushstroke. **Mark: Dog of Fo** for Verreville Pottery, Glasgow. (See Robert Cochran & Co.) £50, $100.

145. Two jugs. c. 7" and 8" (17.8 & 20.3 cm). Sponge printed in mulberry and brown. **No mark,** but identifiable by shape to c. 1850 and Verreville Pottery (1846-1917). £90, $180 & £80, $160.

146. Soup plate. c. 8″ (20.3 cm). Pattern at rim is of three dark green 'asters' with six groups of purple foliage, all painted. There are four sponge printed motifs of quatrefoils joined in pairs by a line all in green. **Mark: POSSIL POTTERY, GLASGOW. See KAD B1911.** £140, $280.

147. Green banded bowl. Between the two bands there are alternate swags in green and bows in pink. The motto is **YOUR E'E IS WAUR TO FILL THAN YOUR WAME** (Your eye is worse to fill than your stomach.) **No mark.** Collection: Hunterian Museum, University of Glasgow. £90, $180.

148. Green-banded bowl. Between the two bands there are two-color prints of thistles. The stamped motto is **NE'ER SCALD YER MOU' WI'ITHER FOLKS KAIL** (Never scald your mouth with other people's kale). **No mark.** £110, $220.

150. Green banded bowl. Between the bands are gold stars and green motifs in two rows. The floor has a stamped thistle and the motto **TOUCH ME IF YOU DARE**. Obviously made for the Scottish market there is yet something in the style of this bowl that sets it apart from most of the others. Even the motto is not in Scots dialect. **No mark.** £150, $300.

149. Green banded bowl. Between the bands are alternate crimson birds and green holly leaves. The stamped motto is **PEACE & GOODWILL** with two black birds. **No mark.** A Christmas present. Collection: Hunterian Museum, University of Glasgow. £150, $300.

151. Green banded bowl. Between the bands are two colored motifs of thistles. On the floor is the motto **CONTENTED WI' LITTLE AND CANTIE WI' MAIR** (Contented with a little and happy with more). **No mark.** £90, $180.

152. Mug. c. 4" (10.5 cm). Two crimson lines. Between them are alternate crowns in blue and crossed flags in crimson and blue. **No mark.** Collection: Hunterian Museum, University of Glasgow. A "patriotic" piece, this time with "French" and "British" flags. £95, $190.

153. Bowl. Decorated in the interior with crimson and blue lines and alternate blue crowns and crimson flags between. The floor has a scene of soldiers running with GORDON HIGHLANDERS underneath and **WE'LL FIGHT AND WE'LL CONQUER AGAIN AND AGAIN** above. This presumably dates from the time of the First World War. It was very popular judging by the number which still remain. **No mark.** Collection: Hunterian Museum, University of Glasgow. £200, $400.

154. Bowl with beaded rim. It has the same transfer print as **no. 153** but in blue and the sponge printing is totally missing. **No mark.** £100, $200.

155. Bowl. Decorated in the interior with a band of blue chains and crimson flowers. The floor has a scene of soldiers marching and the phrase **IT'S A LONG LONG WAY TO TIPPERARY**. **No mark.** This bowl has been attributed to Bo'ness, presumably to the Bridgeness Pottery of C. W. McNay. £100, $200.

156. Bowl. Decorated on the interior with crimson and blue lines between which are alternate blue crowns and crossed 'French' and 'British' flags in crimson and blue with one more on the floor of the bowl beneath the stamped legend **IT'S A LONG LONG WAY TO TIPPERARY**. **No mark.** £150, $300.

157. Bowl. A green/blue line under which is a multicolored sponge print of the British and American flags, very worn. **No mark.** £100, $200.

158. Bowl. c. 9" (22.9 cm). Rim and base bands of a gray floral sponged pattern. Between are crossed flags, also in gray. **No mark.** £90, $180.

159. Bowl with beaded rim. Shaded in brown, it shows a print of a battleship with ADMIRAL JELLICOE'S FLAGSHIP underneath and **BRITANNIA RULES THE WAVES** above. **No mark.** This has no sponge printing but is included since it is a rather rare bowl, like no. 154 but showing this scene. £150, $300.

160. Bowl. A First World War (?) patriotic bowl with crossed flags and crowns in crimson and blue with crimson lining and black lettering. Such bowls are found with other mottoes and scenes. They are almost certainly Scottish in manufacture though the source of the central transfer scenes is debatable. **No mark.** £150, $300.

161. and 162. Vegetable dish. 13 x 6" (33 x 15.2 cm). The famous **GRECIAN** pattern in gray which is its commonest manifestation. **No mark.** £60, $120.

163. Molded bowl. 6 x 3.25" (15.2 x 5.1 cm). Vertical bamboo columns (cf. 164) and an oval cartouche. The rim line is red. The three cartouches have sponge printed "British" and "American" flags. Pieces like this are still found in some numbers in Britain, casting doubt on the supposition that the bowls were designed for the American market. **No mark.** £85, $170.

164. Molded bowl, as no. 163. Red flowers and green foliage. It was bought in Ireland where much of the spongeware has a Scottish origin. **No mark.** £75, $150.

165. and 166. Punch bowl. Sponge printed in brown with a fringed motif round the rim and alternate butterflies and Prince of Wales feathers. Brown lining. Clobbering is in red, green and blue. Amber lustre has been used over most of the sponge printing. **No mark.** Clyde Pottery, Greenock. This attribution is made from the evidence of sherds found during excavation on the site of the Pottery and overwhelmingly on provenance of the pieces. £250, $500 & £250, $500.

167. Cup and saucer. An upper band of sponge printed green motifs, a lower one of red. **Mark: T.R. & Co.** which may be Thomas Rathbone & Co. of Portobello, near Edinburgh. **See KAD B1958.** £200, $400.

The following are put into this section in the full knowledge that they may belong in the English section. However, it is very unusual for any English pottery to mark its wares as Made in Britain; it is much more usual for English wares to be marked Made in England.

168. Bowl. 6.375 x 3.25" (16.2 x 8.3 cm). A blue rim line and green sponge printed motifs. **Mark: MADE IN GREAT BRITAIN.** £90, $180.

170. and 171. Bowl. c. 6.5" (16.5 cm). Decorated all in blue with a sponged, shield-shaped rim motif and 'flowers' with painted 'leaves'. **Mark: stamped a crowned shield with a cockerel and the words BRITISH MADE underneath.** £70, $140.

169. Platter or ashet. 12.5 x 10.5" (31.8 x 26.7 cm). **VIRGINIA** with a red rim line and blue sponged flowers. Daubs of yellow and crude florets in brown have been added. **Mark: MADE IN BRITAIN in a circle round an anchor, identifying this as a mark of the British Anchor Pottery Co., Ltd.** See Mark no. 169A and KAD B366. £80, $160.

169A

172. Bowl. 7.25" (18.4 cm). A crimson rim line from which hangs a band of blue "wheels." **Mark: black stamp MADE IN GREAT BRITAIN.** £40, $80.

England

England was overwhelmingly the prime maker of earthenware of all kinds throughout the nineteenth century. Therefore, we should expect the greatest amount of marked spongeware to be found now would come from that source and that is exactly what we do find. It certainly accounts for a very high proportion of the pieces in the Durrie collection and in other American collections. This probably results from the fact that English manufacturers were the biggest suppliers to the American market but may also be exaggerated by the fact that American collectors have made England the most popular area for their collecting.

The English manufacturers have, in general, produced work of very high quality but the level of invention is not quite so high generally. Even firms which produced the highest quality of work, like Adams, seem to have had a very limited repertoire of themes: a few standard patterns, flowers and little else. But the decoration is bold, the colors are often brilliant and this was what the market demanded. English manufacturers, too, seem to have favored the combination of brushstroke and sponge printing over simple sponge printing, though the latter was also produced in large quantities.

Adams seems to have been one of the most prolific spongeware producers, closely followed by George Jones but the latter was more lax in marking wares with the Pottery's name. The impressed Jones mark is found quite often with a stamped Staffordshire, England, and the Royal Arms but very often the same stamped mark is found with no impressed mark and is often not therefore attributed to George Jones. These two potteries, also, were amongst the biggest producers of wares for southeast Asia and much of their work will be seen in the export section along with Bell, Links and the Dutch potteries.

This section opens with two pieces which show a primitive type of sponge printing though that does not mean that they are particularly early. In fact the Maling piece looks, from the body, rather late than early.

173. and 174. Plate. Sponge printed overall in blue in a fairly primitive pattern. **Impressed mark**: **C. T. MALING**. Collection: Kingussie, the Highland Folk Museum, Highland Council. See KAD B1498. £80, $160.

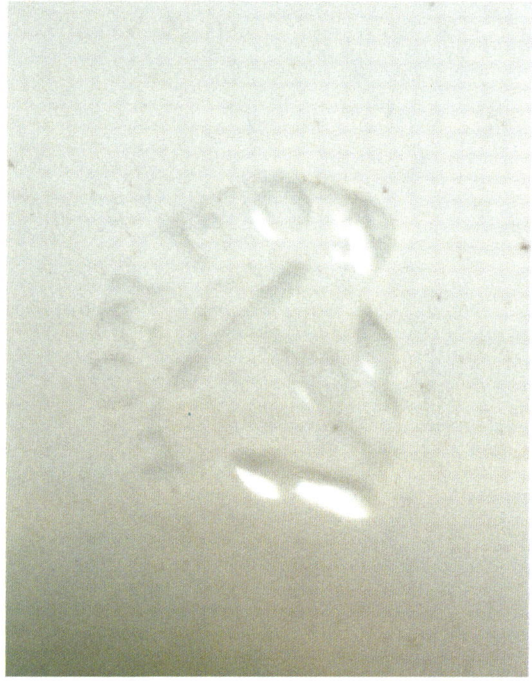

175. and 176. Plate. Sponge printed in blue with a primitive pattern. **Mark: Impressed anchor with an unclear word (perhaps LONDON) above it. See KAD B214.** Collection: Kingussie, Highland Folk Museum, Highland Council. £80, $160.

177A

177. Plate. 9.25" (23.5 cm). The border is sponge printed in black between red lines and the sponged florets are red. The painted center has red, green and blue. **Mark: WM. ADAMS & CO. TUNSTALL ENGLAND and the registration mark for 1881**. This is a derivative of the **GARDEN** pattern. **See Mark 177A.** £120, $240.

178A

178. Tea plate. 6.375" (16.2 cm). **VIRGINIA**. A red flower with purple sepals and blue sponged florets. Sparse green foliage. **Mark: ADAMS, ROYAL IVORY, ENGLAND. See Mark 178A.** £70, $140.

179. Plate. 9.25" (23.5 cm). A green basket weave border with red plums and green foliage. The sponged leaves are dark green and the flower blue. **Mark: WM. ADAMS & CO. and the registration mark for January 21, 1881. See Mark 177A.** £110, $220.

180. Plate. 7.25" (18.4 cm). Yellow lines and yellow and blue "flowers." Blue sponged flowers and green leaves with a central flower in blue and green. **It bears a late ADAMS mark. See Mark 180A.** £75, $150.

180A

181. Cup and saucer. **PERSIAN ROSE** with yellow and green foliage and blue sponged flowers. **Mark: WM. ADAMS & CO. TUNSTALL, ENGLAND**. £50, $100.

182A

182. Platter or ashet. 19.25 x 15" (38.1 x 49.9 cm). **VIRGINIA** variant with red lines. **Mark: WM. ADAMS & CO., TUNSTALL, ENGLAND and registration mark for January 31,1881.** Impressed **IRONSTONE CHINA.** £160, $320.

183. Sugar basin. 6" (15.2 cm). **PERSIAN ROSE** with an added red bud. The sponged flowers are blue. **Mark: WM. ADAMS & CO.** and an illegible registration mark. £100, $200.

184. Cup, saucer and tea plate. Blue lines and blue sponge printed blue balls. Painted foliage in two shades of green and a large red flower. Small, sponge printed red flower. **Mark: WM. ADAMS & CO. TUNSTALL, ENGLAND** and the registration mark for January 21, 1855. **See Mark 177A.** £100, $200.

185. Plate with molded border. 10.25" (26 cm). The lines and foliage are blue, the flowers yellow and green and all are sponge printed. **Mark: CROWN SEMI-PORCELAIN, WM. ADAMS & CO., ENGLAND. See KAD B25.** £85, $170.

185A

186. Cup and saucer in **CAMELLIA**. The rim band and flowers are red, the leaves in two shades of green. **Mark: impressed ADAMS. See KAD B4.** £120, $240.

187. Platter or ashet. 11 x 9" (27.9 x 22.9 cm). A border of blue lines and flow blue poppies with red foliage. The center is also in flow blue with red and green flowers. **Mark: as 181 plus registration mark for January 22, 1883.** £120, $240.

188A

189. Platter or ashet. 10 x 7.25" (25.4 x 18.4 cm). The rim half-flowers are purple, the outer band is green with blue-centered red and yellow flowers at the corners. A central band of the same flowers with green leaves and a blue central flower. **Mark: ADAMS, ENGLAND and impressed IRONSTONE CHINA. See Mark 189A.** £110, $220.

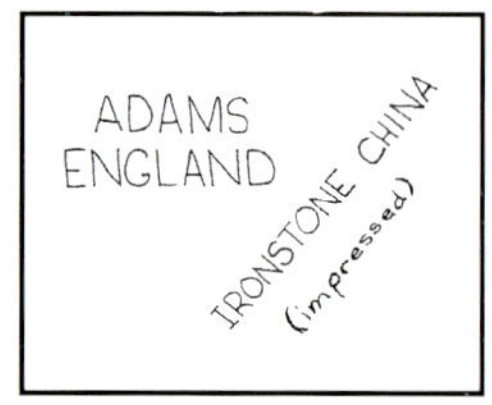

189A

188. Plate. 8.25" (20.9 cm). All in flow blue except the dots which alternate clusters of red and green. **Mark: WM. ADAMS & CO., TUNSTALL and the registration mark for January 21, 1881. See marks 177A & 188A.** £90, $180.

191. Bowl. 5.25 x 2.75" (13.3 x 6.9 cm). Blue and green flower motifs pendant from the rim. Below are pink and green "grapes" and purple and dark green "plums." **Mark: A stag with TRADE MARK above and ADAMS ENGLAND below. See KAD B28.** £90, $180.

190. Plate. 7.375" (18.6 cm). A green basket-weave border. Sponge printed flowers and buds in red and purple with leaves in green. **Mark: WM. ADAMS & CO. TUNSTALL, ENGLAND with the registration mark for January 21, 1868.** £120, $240.

192. Punch bowl with cups. 14 x 7.5" (43.2 x 19.1 cm). Robacker's Christmas "**Bulls-eye**" pattern. **Mark: ADAMS, TUNSTALL**. This is the only marked piece of this pattern so far reported. £400, $800.

193. Bowl. 9.125 x 1.625″ (23.2 x 4.1 cm). An edge dabbed in red with sponge printed blue flowers, yellow centers and green foliage. **Mark: Royal Arms and STAFFORDSHIRE** which may be a George Jones mark. This piece seems to be related to the "careful dabbing" pieces. £40, $80.

194. Plate. 9″ (22.9 cm). All in green. **Mark: GEORGE JONES, STOKE ON TRENT.** £100, $200.

197. Plate. 9.1″ (23.1 cm). All in purple. **Mark: impressed GEORGE JONES, STOKE ON TRENT. See KAD B1389.** £90, $180.

195. and 196. Bowl. 5.375 x 2.625″ (13.7 x 6.7 cm). Flow blue externally and internally. Petra Williams calls this the **REBECCA** pattern and claims it was made by George Jones & Sons. **See KAD B1390.** £50, $100 & £50, $100.

198A

198. Plate. 10" (25.4 cm). Red sponge printed border and center in red, green and blue. **Mark: CRESCENT IVORY above G. J. as monogram above SONS with a crescent. See Mark no. 198A. £110, $220.**

199. Plate. 8.1" (20.5 cm). A blue dabbed edge with a sponge printed floral band in red, green and brown. **Marks: the Royal Arms with ENGLAND and G over a J with SONS in a crescent below for George Jones & Sons. See KAD B1394.** £40, $80.

200. Platter or ashet. Decorated with **PERSIAN ROSE** in blue without sponge printing at all. **MARK: GEORGE JONES AND SONS LTD., STOKE ON TRENT, ENGLAND**. £40, $80.

201. Child's cup. Painted red flowers and green foliage, sponged blue florets and a red line. **Mark: BAKER & COMPANY, ENGLAND**. £50, $100.

202. Plate. 9" (22.9 cm). **PERSIAN ROSE** with an altered crimson flower and crimson line as well as large blue sponge printed flowers and green foliage. **Mark: BAKER & CO. LTD., MADE IN ENGLAND. See Mark no. 202A and KAD B148.** £60, $120.

202A

BAKER & Co L^D
ENGLAND

203. Cup and saucer. Yellow flowers with black centers and small blue flowers. Rim lines are red with red and green foliage. **Mark: OLD ENGLISH, HAND PAINTED, BAKER & CO. ENGLAND. See Mark No. 203A.** £90, $180.

203A

204. Cup and saucer. Black rim lines, yellow sponged flowers and black brushstrokes. **Mark: St. George and the Dragon and OLD ENGLISH, HAND PAINTED, BAKER & CO. LTD. ENGLAND. See Mark No. 203A.** £80, $160.

205. Bowl. 5.375 x 3" (13.7 x 7.6 cm). A blue sponge printed border with red and green painted foliage and red and blue sponged flowers. **Mark: BAKER & CO. LTD., ENGLAND. See Mark No. 202A.** £90, $180.

BAKER & CO. LTD
MADE IN ENGLAND

206A

206. Platter or ashet. 17.75 x 13" (55.1 x 33 cm). Green lines enclose red sponge printed flowers and short green lines. **Mark: BAKER & CO. LTD., MADE IN ENGLAND. See Mark No. 206A.** £160, $320.

207. Child's cup and saucer. A brown line, green foliage, red flowers. **Mark: impressed ELSMORE** & **FOSTER, TUNSTALL. See Mark No. 207A.** £50, $100.

ELSMORE & FOSTER
TUNSTALL

207A

208. Plate. 9.75" (24.7 cm). The band and lines in purple. The leaves are sponge printed in green with black centers. **Mark: impressed ELSMORE & FORSTER. See Mark no. 208A.** £60, $120.

ELSMORE &
FOSTER

208A

209. Plate. As no. 208 but the band and lines are blue and the sponge printing is red with blue centers. **Mark: as above.** £60, $120.

210. Octagonal platter or ashet. 10.25 x 13.5" (26 x 34.3 cm). Blue lines, green and purple leaves and an inner band in purple. **Mark: ELSMORE & FORSTER.** £140, $280.

211. Octagonal platter or ashet. 9.5 x 12.25" (24.1 x 31.1 cm). A close match of the previous piece with a green central band and **mark as above**. £140, $280.

212. Pitcher or ewer. 10" (25.4 cm). Blue lining, red printed holly with green leaves and a band of red foliage. This is unmarked but other pieces are said by Durrie to have been seen with this pattern and **marked ELSMORE & FORSTER, TUNSTALL. See Mark no. 207A.** £130, $260

213. Plate. 8.5" (21.6 cm). Flow blue throughout. **Mark: EDGE, MALKIN & CO. See KAD B823.** £100, $200.

214. Plate. 9" (22.9 cm). Red lines, swags and sponge printed florets. Green foliage and the "Flowers" at the apices are blue. **Mark: impressed EDGE, MALKIN & CO.** £95, $190.

215. Plate. 9" (22.9 cm). Three yellow lines. The outer band has green leaves alternating with red motifs; the inner band is in dark green. **Mark: impressed EDGE, MALKIN & CO.** £110, $220.

216A

216. Child's cup and saucer. **VIRGINIA**. The sepals are blue as are the sponge printed florets. The rest is red and green. **Mark: ALLERTON'S PERSIAN WARE, ENGLAND. See Mark no. 216A.** £55, $110.

217. Sugar basin. 4.5" high (11.4 cm). The edges are dabbed in blue. The other motifs are sponge printed in red, green and blue. **Mark: ALLERTON'S PERSIAN WARE, ENGLAND, as above.** £60, $120.

218A

218. Rice dish. 10 x 1.75" (25.4 x 4.4 cm). **VIRGINIA** with flowers and sponged florets in lavender. **Mark: POWELL & BISHOP, ENGLAND**. Is this possibly an export piece? **See Mark no. 218A.** £75, $150

219. Plate. 9.875" (25.2 cm). A loose-textured sponge print in green. **Mark: POWELL & BISHOP, IRONSTONE CHINA, AMERICAN SHAPE (1876-8).** £40, $80.

220. Bowl. 7 x 3.5" (17.8 x 8,8 cm). A red band between green lines. Red sponged stars and blue sponged flowers, green painted leaves. **Mark: JAMES REEVES, STOKE ON TRENT MADE IN ENGLAND. See Mark no. 220A.** £60, $120.

220A

221. Bowl. 6.75 x 2.625" (17.1 x 6.7 cm). **PERSIAN ROSE** with a red rim line. **Mark: JAMES REEVES, STOKE ON TRENT, MADE IN ENGLAND.** £60, $120.

222. Bowl. Rim band of red sponged motifs and blue sponged flowers with painted green leaves. **Mark: JAMES REEVES, STOKE ON TRENT, MADE IN ENGLAND.** £80, $160.

223. Child's cup, saucer and plate. A red rim line and black diamonds. **Mark: impressed DAVENPORT and anchor. Before 1882. See Mark no. 223A.** £140, $280

223A

224. Child's tea set. Black lines, red flowers, green leaves. **Mark: an impressed anchor and DAVENPORT. Mark as above.** £300, $600.

225. Plate. 9.5" (24.1 cm). A loosely textured print. The border bands are red, then there are two rows of green separated by two yellow lines round a blue one, overprinted with a black sponge print. Two blue lines enclose a blank center. **Mark: an impressed anchor and perhaps DAVENPORT**. £200, $400.

226. Soup plate. 7.75″ (19.7 cm). The flange has a red line and blue sponged motifs; the lower band is in red. **Mark: impressed anchor and DAVENPORT, as above**. £150, $300.

227. Plate. 9.5″ (24.1 cm). A red line, an outer green band and an inner red band. **Mark: CLEMENTSON BROTHERS, HANLEY. See Mark no. 227A.** £80, $160.

227A

228. Saucer. 6″ (15.2 cm). All in brown. **Mark: a phoenix with CLEMENTSON BROTHERS, ENGLAND below. See Mark no. 227A.** £30, $60.

229. Plate. 7.5″ (19.1 cm). A sponge printed border in blue and a blue transfer print. This is sometimes called ***EMBASSY CHINA*** or ***CONSULATE CHINA*** since some pieces marked **U.S. CONSULATE SERVICE 1868** are known; but, the name should be kept to such pieces since the backstamp reveals that the pattern name is **GEM**, the Maker R. HAMMERSLEY and the registry date April 23, 1868. The print is also known in purple. **See Mark no. 229A.** £200, $400.

229A

230. Bowl. 6.375 x 3.5″ (16.2 x 8.9 cm). Black lines. An upper band of sponge printing is red and the lower green. **Mark: inscribed in red H. A. & C. L. ENGLAND** - probably H. Aynsley & CO., Commercial Works, Longton, Staffs. **See Mark no. 230A.** £90, $180.

230A

231. Plate. 8.75″ (22 cm). All sponge printed and lined. The outer band is of red daisies. The next row is of blue bows and the inner row is green. **Mark: impressed BARLOW, LONGTON. See Mark no. 231A.** £120, $240.

231A

232. Rice dish. 9.625″ x 1.75″ (24.2 x 4.4 cm). All in flow blue except for the very small middle band where the motifs are alternately red and green. **Mark: impressed J. & G. MEAKIN. See KAD B1602.** £100, $200

233. Bowl. 4.5″ (11.4 cm). A black, sponge printed reticulated pattern. **Mark: impressed J. & G. MEAKIN**, a Hanley firm. The pattern is also known in blue. £65, $130.

234 and 235. Invalid's spit pot. 7″ x 8.5″ (17.8 x 21.6 cm). Sponge printed bands of red and green. **Mark: a printed rectangle with T. B. & SONS over FB**. Probably Thomas Booth & Son, Church Bank Pottery, Tunstall (1872-6) according to Durrie. £130, $260 & £130, $260.

236. Plate. 9″ (22.9 cm). Groups of sponged red leaves and blue flowers with green painted foliage. **Mark: impressed EDGE MALKIN & CO. See KAD B823.** £100, $200.

237. Plate. 9″ (22.9 cm). A complex sponge of red, green and blue. **Mark: in a circle ELINON UNDER GLAZE HAND PAINTED and PRICE in the center. See Mark no. 237A.** £50, $100.

237A

239. Pitcher. 5″ (12.7 cm). Red and black lines with painted green leaves, sponge printed red flowers, dots and blue buds. **Mark: ADDERLEYS, MADE IN ENGLAND.** £40, $80.

238. Bowl. 5.5 x 3.125″ (14 x 7.9 cm). A black rim line and black and yellow lines near the base. Between are two large painted green flowers with yellow centers and black and green foliage with blue and yellow sponge printed flowers. **Mark: ADDERLEYS, MADE IN ENGLAND**. **See Mark no. 238A.** £45, $90.

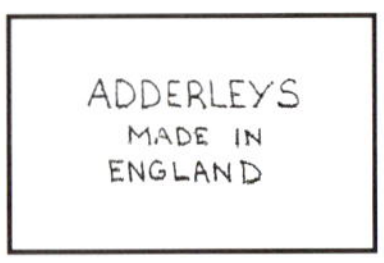

238A

240. Bowl. 6.75 x 3.75″ (17.1 x 9.5 cm). **VIRGINIA** with purple sponged flowers. **Mark: T. G. GREEN & CO. LTD. CHURCH GRESLEY, MADE IN ENGLAND. See Mark no. 240A.** £40, $80.

240A

241. Platter or ashet. **VIRGINIA** with violet sponged elements. **Mark: OAKVILLE, T.G. GREEN & CO. Ltd. CHURCH GRESLEY, MADE IN ENGLAND.** £60, $120.

242. Bowl. **VIRGINIA** with violet sponged elements. **Mark: GREEN & CO. Ltd. GRESLEY, ENGLAND.** £70, $140.

243. Cup and saucer. Flow blue. **Mark: Royal Arms with H.O. EDMISTON, ENGLAND**. **See Mark no. 243A.** £100, $200.

243A

244. Cup and saucer. Bands in black, blue and green. Each panel has red sponge printed flowers and light green foliage. Other decoration is dark green. **Mark: the Royal Arms and ENGLAND**. Similar plates in other colors are known with the mark **H. O., EDMISTON**. £120, $240.

245. Plate. 9" (22.9 cm). A green dabbed edge and sponge printed sprays of foliage. **No mark** but similar pieces are known **marked S.C. & CO.** perhaps for Steven Clive, Well St., Pottery, Tunstall (1875-1889). £40, $80.

246. Bowl. **PERSIAN ROSE** with blue sponge printed 'flowers'. **Mark: PRIMAVESI & SON CARDIFF on a ribbon with a crown**. Primavesi was a dealer who had wares made for him. The likelihood is that this is English in origin. **See Mark no. 246A.** £60, $120.

246A

The following all are marked Staffordshire, England or Staffs. England with usually no further clue to their origin.

247. Plate. 6.875" (17.5 cm). A red rim line and painted flowers with green foliage and blue sponged florets. Obviously a derivative of **PERSIAN ROSE**. **Mark: STAFFORDSHIRE, ENGLAND**. £60, $120.

248. Plate. 9.125" (23.2 cm). **PERSIAN ROSE** with green and blue foliage and yellow sponged florets. **Mark: STAFFORDSHIRE, ENGLAND.** £60, $120.

249. Bowl. 4.75 x 2.875" (12.1 x 7.2 cm). Green lines, yellow flowers both sponged and painted and black foliage. **Mark: rampant horses flanking an oval and STAFFORDSHIRE, ENGLAND**. Probably George Jones & Sons. £60, $120.

250. Plate. 9" (22.9 cm). **PERSIAN ROSE. Mark: an anchor with a central B and flanking lions with STAFFORDSHIRE, ENGLAND**, i.e. the British Anchor CO. **See Mark no. 250A.** £60, $120.

250A

251. Plate. 8.875" (22.4 cm). A blue rim line and sponge printed dot flowers with red stems. The leaves are painted in green. **Mark: Lion and unicorn above STAFFORDSHIRE, ENGLAND and an indecipherable mark.** £65, $130.

252. Bowl. 5.75 x 3" (14.6 x 7.6 cm). **VIRGINIA** variant with a red rim line. **Mark: as 251**. £60, $120.

253. Bowl. 6.375 x 3.375" (16.2 x 8.6 cm). Red lines at the rim enclose sponged black squares. The large flowers are sponge printed in blue and the foliage is green. **Mark: STAFFORDSHIRE, ENGLAND.** £70, $140.

254. Bowl. 7.25 x 3.625" (18.4 x 9.2 cm). **PERSIAN ROSE** with blue sponge printed flowers. **Mark: rampant lions flanking an oval with an anchor and STAFFORDSHIRE, ENGLAND. See Mark no. 250A.** £60, $120.

255. Bowl. 7.25 x 3.5" (18.4 x 8.9 cm). Large red sponge printed flowers and smaller blue with green leaves along a black line. **Mark: rampant lions flank an oval with an anchor and the letter B and STAFFORDSHIRE, ENGLAND**. Used by the British Anchor Pottery, Anchor Rd., Longton. £60, $120.

256. Saucer. 6" (15.2 cm). A red line, then a band of alternating red and blue flowers with yellow centers, green foliage. **Mark: the Royal Arms with STAFFORDSHIRE, ENGLAND**. One plate has the inscription **FROM LIZZIE BRYON TO EDITHA A. WALKER CHRISTMAS 1895**. **See Mark no. 256A.** £50, $100.

257. Plate. 8.625" (21.9 cm). The rim and flowers are in red, the leaves in two shades of green with a brown connecting line. **Mark: the Royal Arms and STAFFORDSHIRE, ENGLAND**. **See Mark no. 256A.** £80, $160.

256A

258. Child's cup and saucer. Brown rim lines and blue/green sponge printed motifs. **Mark: STAFFORDSHIRE, ENGLAND. See Mark no. 256A.** £80, $160.

259. Child's tea service from a 20 piece set. Green lines and red diamonds. **Mark: STAFFORDSHIRE, ENGLAND**. (cf. above entry, 258). **See Mark no. 256A.** £200, $400.

260. Child's tea service. Brown lines and blue sponge printed motifs. **Mark: Royal Arms** and **ENGLAND.** £80, $160.

261. Bowl. 5.625 x 3" (14.3 x 7.6 cm). Broad blue bands flanked by red lines. Between are sponged red flowers. **Mark: the Royal Arms with an anchor overlaid by a B and STAFFORDSHIRE, ENGLAND**. Again, the British Anchor Co. **See Mark no. 250A.** £60, $120.

262. Plate. 9" (22,9 cm). A red rim line and **VIRGINIA** with red joining lines and purple sponged "stars." **Mark: MADE IN ENGLAND**. £60, $120.

263. Plate. 8.875" (22.4 cm). **VIRGINIA** with a black rim line. The flower is dark brown with yellow "falls;" the leaves are dark brown and the sponge printed flowers yellow. **Mark: MADE IN ENGLAND round an anchor.** £90, $180.

264. Rice dish. 10 x 2.125″ (25.4 x 5.4 cm). A red line and large red flowers (including the central one), the sponged flowers are blue and the foliage green. **Mark: MADE IN ENGLAND**. £80, $160.

265. Rice dish. 8″ x 1.875″ (20.3 x 4.8 cm). Red lines and sponged flowers, dark green painted flowers and green foliage. **Mark: MADE IN ENGLAND**. £80, $160.

266. Rice dish. 10″ (25.4 cm). **GARDEN**. A black sponged border between crimson lines. Three painted flares in yellow. Red sponge printed flowers with brown painted foliage. The central flower is blue and brown with a red line. **Mark: MADE IN ENGLAND**. £60, $120.

267. Bowl. 9.5 x 4.75″ (24.1 x 12.1 cm). **PERSIAN ROSE** with red lines. **Mark: HAND PAINTED, MADE IN ENGLAND. See Mark no. 267A.** £65, $130.

267A

268. Bowl. 6 x 3.3″ (15.2 x 8.5 cm). A red rim line and black central connecting line. Red, sponge printed single flowers and clustered blue. Green leaves. **Mark: MADE IN ENGLAND**. £80, $160.

269. Serving plate with divisions. 11″ (27.9 cm). Lines and sponged stars in blue, painted red flares and green foliage. **Mark: MADE IN ENGLAND**. £50, $100.

270. Bowl. 5.875 x 3.75″ (14.9 x 9.5 cm). A red line, painted yellow flowers, dark green foliage and blue sponged flowers. **Mark: MADE IN ENGLAND**. £55, $110.

271. Bowl. 6.25 x 3.25″ (15.9 x 8.3 cm). Red lines and sponge printed flowers, green sponge printed foliage. **Mark: rampant horses flanking an oval and STAFFORDSHIRE, ENGLAND**. Perhaps by George Jones. **See Mark no. 271A.** £80, $160.

271A

272. Bowl. Yellow painted flowers with yellow and red foliage and green sponge printed motifs all on a central green line. **Mark: MADE IN ENGLAND in a rectangle, stamped**. £60, $120.

273. Cup and saucer. Purple rim lines, red sponged flowers and paired blue dots. Green foliage. **Mark: the Royal Arms and ENGLAND**. £60, $120.

274. Cup and saucer. A brown line and dot flowers with green foliage. **Mark: the Royal Arms with ENGLAND.** £60, $120.

275. Plate. 9" (22.9 cm). A red rim line and sponged flowers with black painted stems and green leaves. **Mark: ENGLAND in a rectangle. See Mark no. 275A.** £70, $140.

275A

276. Cup and saucer. Blue lines, yellow flowers and red foliage. **Mark: the Royal Arms and ENGLAND**. £30, $60.

277. Cup. All in red. **Mark: ENGLAND**. £30, $60.

278. Saucer. 6.125" (15.7 cm). A broad blue band and a narrow red line. The sponge printed motifs are black. **Mark: the Royal Arms and ENGLAND**. £90, $180.

279. Cup, saucer and plate. Red lines and blue diamonds. **Mark: the Royal Arms and ENGLAND** plus an impressed crescent with illegible letters. George Jones? £80, $160.

280. Plate. 6.5" (16.2 cm). All in deep blue. **Mark: the Royal Arms and ENGLAND plus an impressed D with a crescent.** £90, $180.

281. Bowl. 6.375 x 3.5" (16.2 x 8.8 cm). Brown lines with an upper red band and lower blue band of sponge printed flowers. **Mark: ENGLAND**. £50, $100.

282. Cup and saucer. Blue lines and large purple motifs with small yellow ones. **Mark: the Royal Arms and ENGLAND.** £70, $140.

283. Bowl. 6.75 x 3.75" (17.1 x 9.5 cm). A central blue band and four yellow lines with red sponge printed motifs. **Mark: MADE IN ENGLAND.** £100, $200.

284. Cheese dish. Blue lines, green and red sponge printed motifs. **Mark: a lamp and ENGLAND**. £80, $160.

285. Bowl. 6" x 3" (15.2 x 7.6 cm). Red lines with an upper sponge printed band in blue and a lower in red. **Mark: the Royal Arms and ENGLAND.** £40, $80.

286. Plate. 8.5" (21.6 cm). A blue line. The sponge printed decoration alternates red and blue. **Mark: the Royal Arms above ENGLAND, an impressed crescent and an illegible letter**, perhaps George Jones. £80, $160.

287. Rice dish. 10.375 x 2.25" (26.4 x 5.7 cm). Red lines and flowers with foliage in two shades of green, and blue sponged "stars" which are almost invisible in the photograph. **Mark: a crowned globe with M and G on opposite sides. See Mark no. 287A.** £80, $160.

287A

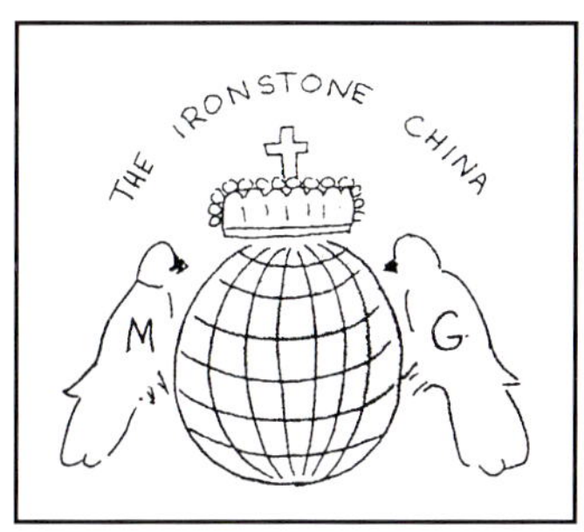

288. Rice dish. A travesty of **VIRGINIA** with the same mark as the last entry, 287. £90, $180.

289. Platter or ashet. 16 x 12.625″ (41.6 x 22.1 cm). Dark green lines and foliage with painted and sponged flowers, both yellow. **Mark: anchor with MADE IN GREAT BRITAIN round it.** £120, $240.

Titian Ware

Made by Adams, Titian Ware has no right to a place in a book on spongeware. It was included in the Durrie collection, presumably under the impression that it was decorated by sponge printing but in fact this is seldom if ever the case. Even Titian Ware marks stress that it is 'hand-painted'. Occasionally there may be a slight element of sponge printing in a piece **(see 301)** but this is rare. The name really refers to a honey-colored glaze which was used on an ivory body which was very fashionable in the early years of the twentieth century and used by many other potteries. The following illustrations are included mainly to illustrate the difference between spongeware and Titian Ware.

290. Plate. 6″ (15.2 cm). Purple berries and red flowers. **Mark: ROYAL IVORY ENGLAND TITIAN WARE and the registration mark No. 489174 (for 1906). See Mark no. 290A.** £150, $300.

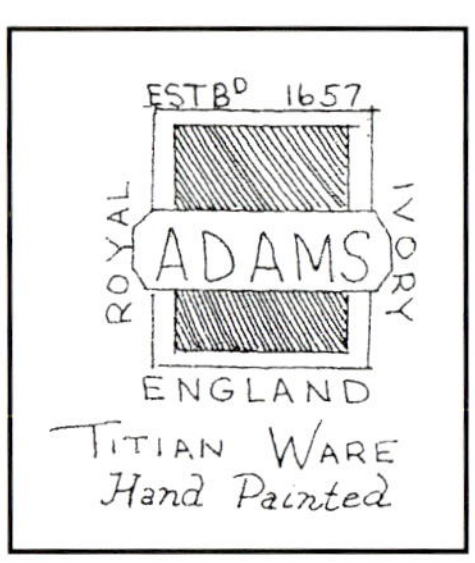

290A

291. Plate. 9″ (22.9 cm). Brown lines, green foliage and sponge printed red flowers. **Mark: as 290 but with a different reg. no.** £250, $500.

292. Tea service. Green lines and foliage, red and yellow flowers. **Printed registration number 673892 (after 1909).** £120, $240.

293. Plate. 8″ (20.3 cm). Red flowers with green foliage, purple, red and blue flowers. **Mark: as 290A but without reg. no.** £110, $220.

294. Bowl. 6″ x 4″ (15.2 x 10.2 cm). Green lines and foliage with brown flowers and buds. **Mark: as above.** £100, $200.

295. Cup and saucer. Red lines and flowers with green foliage and blue flowers. **Mark: as 290A plus HAND PAINTED and ALCAZAR. Registration Number 459174 (for 1905).** £150, $300.

296. Plate. 12.5″ (31.8 cm). Lines in blue and green combine with motifs in red and green. **Mark: as 290A**. In view of its size, it seems likely that this piece was meant as a wall plaque rather than a dinner plate. £110, $220.

297. Platter or ashet. 13.5 x 10.625″ (34.3 x 27 cm). Broad yellow lines, a narrow blue line and two other bands. **Mark: as 290A plus TITIAN WARE**. £90, $180.

298. Plate. 6″ (15.2 cm). Green lines and foliage with red flowers. **Mark: as above plus registration number 456174 (for 1905).** £90, $180.

299. Plate. 9″ (22.9 cm). Blue and yellow flowers and buds with green stems and foliage. **Mark: as above plus MEXICO.** £80, $160.

300. Plate. 9.875" (25.1 cm). A brown rim line and an inner green one. Green foliage and flowers in blue with yellow centers and in yellow with brown centers. **Mark: as above plus LAKEWOOD and 595858 for c. 1912.** £50, $100.

301. Several pieces of **Titian Ware**, one of which has a version of **PERSIAN ROSE** with a sponge printed element. £65, $130.

Holland

Holland has an important place in the history of spongeware. Like Britain it had an empire still in the nineteenth and at the beginning of the twentieth century and this became a ready market for its wares, including ceramics, in which, of course, Holland had a proud place.

The two main manufacturers of spongeware were the Sphinx Pottery of Petrus Regout and the Société Cêramique. It has often been stated that these were the same firm and so they were after 1958. But at that date they had both long given up the making of spongeware, so for our purposes they are different firms. The Sphinx Pottery was set up in 1836 in Maastricht; their main period of spongeware production is said to have been 1890-1914. The Société Cêramique made spongeware mainly between 1920 and 1940, according to a catalogue for an exhibition held in Maastricht but this seems rather late.

If the dates given are correct even approximately then it seems likely that both businesses were stimulated to create their best spongeware following the success of British potteries in the southeast Asian market. As will be seen in a later section, both of the Maastricht potteries had great success with wares destined for this market.

302. Bowl. 9.625 x 3.75" (24.4 x 9.5 cm). Black lines, painted green leaves and sponged flowers and half-flowers in red, yellow and blue with yellow centers. **Mark: PETRUS REGOUT, MAASTRICHT, MADE IN HOLLAND. See Mark no. 302A**. £65, $130.

302A

303. Cup and saucer. Sponged yellow florets, painted red lines and red and blue large flowers with dark green leaves. **Mark as above.** £75, $150.

304. Bowl. 5″ x 3.25″ (12.7 x 8.3 cm). All in flow blue. Inside are sponged motifs, the exterior is painted. **Mark: as previous entry, but with alternative spelling "MAESTRICHT".** Proof that "Scottish flow blue" was not all made in Scotland. £80, $160.

304A

305. Plate. 9.125″ (23.2 cm). A red sponged border. Yellow lines enclose flares in blue and yellow, green foliage and sponged blue flowers. **Mark: as previous entries except that the town is spelt MAESTRICHT.** £60, $120.

306. Cup and saucer. The leaves and flowers are sponge printed, the rest is painted. **See Mark no. 302A.** £50, $100.

307. Pitcher. 6.5" (16.5 cm). A red rim line and a blue sponge printed band above **PERSIAN ROSE** with blue sponged flowers - all below the spout. **Mark: SOCIÉTÉ CÊRAMIQUE, MAESTRICHT, MADE IN HOLLAND. See Mark no. 307A and KAD C134.** £70, $140.

307A

308. Platter or ashet. 12.25 x 9.125" (31.1 x 23.2 cm). A red rim line and flowers, both painted and sponge printed. Green foliage. **Mark: SOCIÉTÉ CÊRAMIQUE, MAESTRICHT, HOLLAND**. - Mark variation noted without **"MADE IN HOLLAND".** £90, $180.

310. Plate. 9" (22.9 cm). A red line and sponge printed border with painting in purple, yellow, green and black. **Mark: as above**. £60, $120.

309. Bowl. 6 x 3.25" (15.2 x 8.3 cm). Sponged leaves hang from the rim and sponged flowers on the bottom have painted leaves. **Mark: as above**. £80, $160.

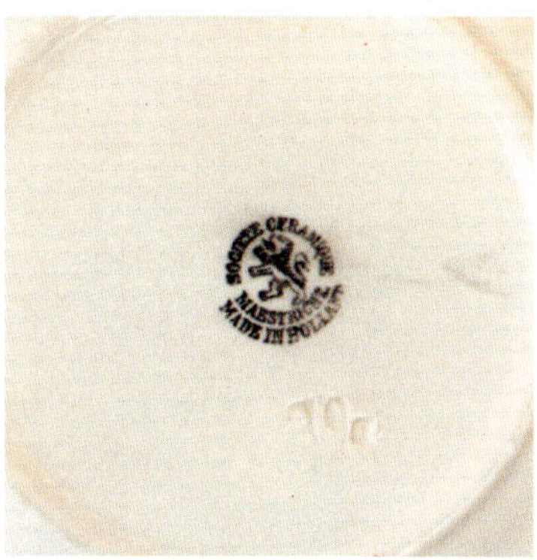

309A

311. Plate. 9.15" (23.3 cm). A red rim line, red and green foliage and large yellow flowers with black sponge printed centers. **Mark: SOCIÉTÉ CÊRAMIQUE**. £100, $200.

312. Plate. 8.625" (21.9 cm). Red lines and plums. Light green painted and dark green sponged foliage with blue florets. This plate could have been intended as an export piece, and perhaps was. **Mark: SOCIÉTÉ CÊRAMIQUE.** £60, $120.

313. Bowl. 4.375 x 2.5" (11.1 x 6.3 cm). **VIRGINIA** with blue sponged flowers. **Mark: as above**. £100, $200.

314. Rice dish. 9.25" (23.2 cm). **GARDEN**. Sponge printed daisies but all else is painted. **Mark: as above.** £100, $200.

315. Rice dish. 9 x 1.2″ (22.9 x 3 cm). **GARDEN**. A blue sponged border and small red sponged flowers. The flares are red and the central flower red and green. **Mark: as above**. £65, $130.

316. Rice dish. 9″ (22.9 cm). **VIRGINIA** with a red rim line and purple sponge printed flowers. **Mark: as above.** £80, $160.

317. Plate. 8.75″ (22 cm). **GARDEN**. Yellow lines and blue and green central flower. **Mark: as above.** £130, $260.

318. Coffee pot. 8″ (20.3 cm). **GARDEN** adapted to a very different shape. Durrie gives **No mark** for this but has included it amongst the Sociéte Cêramique pieces and pointed out its identity in pattern with **no. 307.** £90, $180.

319. Plate. 9″ (22.0 cm). **GARDEN** with only a narrow sponge printed border. The central flower is blue and green within yellow. **Mark: SOCIÉTÉ CÊRAMIQUE**. £150, $300.

320. Plate. 9″ (22.9 cm). The plum pattern with a red sponge printed border. **Mark: as above.** £70, $140.

321. Bowl. 9.5 x 5″ (24.1 x 12.7 cm). A black rim line, blue sponged flowers with red centers, painted red and green flowers and four blue, sponged petals. Red sponged foliage and painted foliage on the bottom of the interior. **Mark: SOCIÉTÉ CÊRAMIQUE, MAESTRICHT, MADE IN HOLLAND**. **See Mark no. 307A.** £80, $160.

322. Plate. 9″ (22.9 cm). Thin purple lines enclose two bands of sponge printed diamonds in fours. The florets are alternately red and green. **Mark: SOCIÉTÉ CÊRAMIQUE, MAESTRICHT, MADE IN HOLLAND. See Mark no. 307A.** £70, $140.

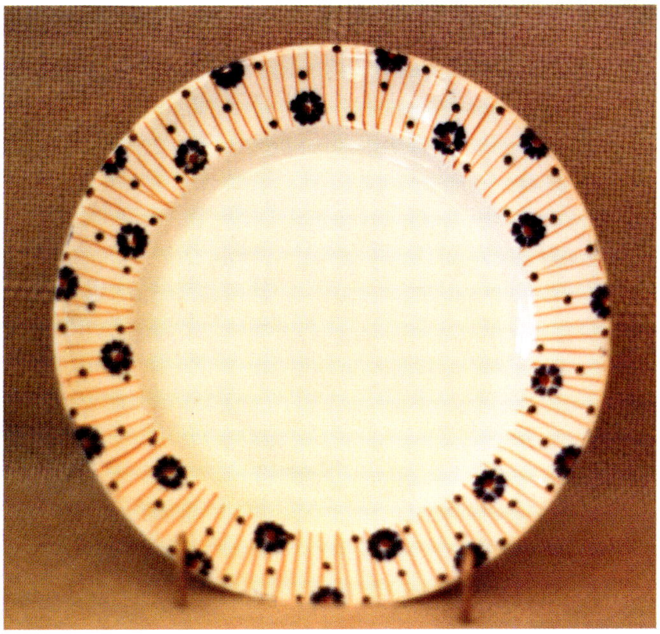

323. Plate with molded flange. 8.625" (21.9 cm). Ochre lines and blue sponge printed flowers with red centers. Green dots. **See Mark no. 307A.** £50, $100.

324. Bowl. 4.1 x 2.5" (10.4 x 6.3 cm). Black lines and red and green sponge printed motifs. **See Mark no. 307A.** £50, $100.

325. Bowl. 3.1 x 2" (7.8 x 5.1 cm). Lines in black, red and green and a yellowish brown band with black sponged cross-centered diamonds overprinted. **Mark: as above**. £120, $240.

326. Rice dish. 10.5" (26.5 cm). **GARDEN** in crimson, blue, black and brown. **Usual Société Cêramique mark. See Mark no. 307A.** Bought in Scotland**.** £80, $160.

France

Most of the French pieces seem to take the form of plates with a simple, sponge printed border and a painted scene, usually with one or two figures on the floor of the plate.

327. Bowl. 7.875 x 2.125" (20 x 5.4 cm). Decorated on the concave surface. Red lines, painted flowers in red and blue, pale green and purple sponged flowers. **Mark: a rampant animal in the center with indistinct French - DE LA FAIENCERIE DE ? ANCI MOUZIN LECAT ET CIE. See Mark no. 327A and KAD C16A.** £90, $180.

327A

328. Bowl. 10 x 3.375" (25.4 x 8.6 cm). A red sponge printed border and a multicolored painted center with a bagpipe player. **Mark: Swan in a circle. Round it NOUVELLES CERAMIQUES DU NORD ST. AMANS. See Mark no. 328A.** - See *Zuhlsdorff*, p. 598 and Mark 11.249 p. 321, c. 1908. £100, $200.

328A

329. Plate. 7.5" (19.1 cm). A blue sponge printed border, a large red and yellow flower with red and blue flowers and green foliage. **Mark: FRANCE**. £100, $200.

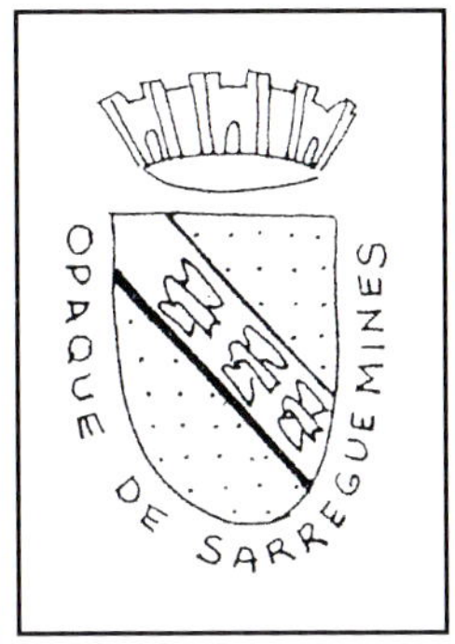

330A

330-331. Bowl on a metal frame. All blue with sponge printed flowers. There is a red cord interwoven in the metal. **Mark: OPAQUE DE SARREGUEMINES. See Mark no. 330A and KAD C44.** £90, $180.

332. Cup and saucer. Flow blue but the sponged flowers have red or yellow crescents. **Mark: a crowned shield and OPAQUE DE SARREGUEMINES. See Mark no. 330A.** £100, $200.

333. Plate. Crimson sponge printed border with multi-colored central man in landscape. **Mark: NORD MOULINS DES LOUPS ET HAMAGE FRANCE.** £1000, $2000.

334. Plate. 9" (22.9 cm). A red sponge printed border and red, green, yellow and black painting in the center. (Mouzin Lecat & Co.) **Mark: a crowned shield and wreath with OPAQUE LUNEVILLE FRANCE. See Mark no. 334A.** £75, $150.

333A

334A

336. Plate. 8.5" (21.6 cm). Lines and sponge printed flowers in red, painting in yellow, black, green and blue. **Mark: a crowned shield and BOCH. LA LOUVIERE. See Mark no. 336A and KAD C11.** £100, $200.

336A

335. Soup plate. 10.1" (25.6 cm). A red sponged border and a center painted in red, green, blue, brown and yellow with a woman knitting. **Mark: a windmill and NORD MOULIN DE LOUPS ET HAMAGE.** See *Zuhlsdorff*, p. 598, Mark 2.2304, p. 214, c. 1920s-1930s. £80, $160.

335A

338. Soup plate. 10.125" (25.7 cm). Red lines enclose a blue sponge printed border. The peacock center is multicolored. **Mark: PORCELAINE OPAQUE DIGUIN. See Mark no. 338A.** £90, $180.

338A

337. Bowl. 10.25 x 2.75" (26 x 6.9 cm). The flow blue is all brushstroke except for the clusters of three florets. **Mark: a crowned shield and SARREGUEMINES ET DIGUIN, FRANCE. See Mark no. 337A.** £60, $120.

337A

339. Plate. 8.75" (22 cm). Large yellow flowers and foliage in two shades of green, blue and red with sponged florets in blue. **Mark: a crowned shield and illegible words with MADE IN FRANCE. See Mark no. 332A.** £90, $180.

340. Platter or ashet. 12 x 8.5″ (30.5 x 21.6 cm). A blue, sponge printed border with a center painted in red, green, blue and yellow. **Mark: a crowned shield with ST. AMAND ETABLISSEMENTS CERAMIQUES, MADE IN FRANCE. See Mark no. 333A.** £100, $200.

341. Bowl. 9 x 2″ (22.9 x 5.1 cm). Flow blue with four clusters of sponge printed flowers. **Mark: a crowned shield with OPAQUE DE SARREGUEMINES. See Mark no. 330A.** £60, $120.

342. Bowl with exterior fluting. A blue, sponge printed border in the interior and a stencilled central figure with a dog in black, clobbered in red, blue and yellow. The foliage is dabbed green. **On the base is FRANCE**. Matching bowls are recorded with mark **ST. C. FRANCE**. **See Mark no. 342A.** £60, $120.

342A

343. Cup and saucer. Red lines and red and green sponge printed motifs. **Mark: SARREGUEMINES with a crown above and SARREGUEMINES ET DIGOIN around a shield of France below.** **See Mark no. 337A.** £70, $140.

344. Bowl. 4.5 x 2.5″ (11.4 x 6.3 cm). Black lines enclose a red band. Below is a band of blue sponge printing. **Mark: A crowned shield with OPAQUE DE SARREGUEMINES. See Mark no. 330A.** £90, $180.

345. Bowl. 9 x 1.75″ (22.9 x 4.4 cm). A green sponged border. Stencilled red flower, blue dots and green foliage. The greeting would indicate a gift plate made in Central Europe, most probably Germany. **No mark.** £80, $160.

346. Plate or wall plaque. 11″ (27.9 cm). Black lines enclose a red sponged border. The center is painted in red, green, blue and purple. **Mark: impressed WILHELMSBURG. See Mark no. 346A.** See *Rontgen*, pp. 504-505 and *Zuhlsdorff*, pp. 203-204 and 649. £85, $170.

346A 

347. Soup plate. 9″ (22.9 cm). Red lines enclose a blue sponge printed border. The center is stencilled. **Mark: AMBERG**. See *Zuhlsdorff*, p. 393, mark 2.63, p. 124. £85, $170.

348 and 349. Note: There are no Figures 348 and 349 in this text.

350. Pitcher. 7" (17.8 cm). Black handle and lines. Painted blue flowers with red, green and yellow centers. **Mark: stamped GEZ. GESCH, GERMANY**. A companion vase has an impressed stag in a circle as well. **See Mark no. 350A.** £50, $100.

351 Child's cup and saucer. A green sponged border is separated by a yellow line from a blue sponged band with a painted fringe. The central green band is like the border. **Mark: impressed GERMANY**. £110, $220.

350A

352. Bowl. 4.5" (11.4 cm). Sponged green leaves and red strawberries and painted black dots. **Mark: GERMANY**. £40, $80.

353. Cream jug, sugar basin and plate (7" or 17.8 cm). This pattern has also been found as a child's tea set. **Mark: a crowned shield with MADE IN GERMANY and the pattern name STUART** (cf. 99). £40, $80.

354. Plate. 6.875" (17.5 cm). All in blue. **Mark an impressed shield flanked by A. & S. with L. below and GERMANY. Unidentified potter. See Mark no. 354A.** £50, $100.

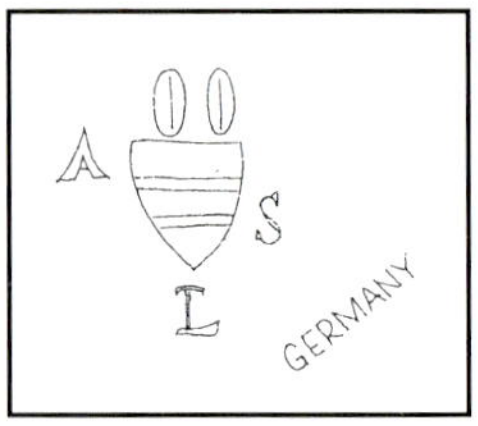

354A

355. Bowl. 7.5 x 3.25" (19.1 x 8.3 cm). Red and blue motifs with dots. **Mark: a large crowned A with A. & G. above an S. Below is DEKOR 602 and GERMANY. See Mark no. 355A.** See *Zuhlsdorff*, p. 467, mark 1.2373 p. 111, c. 1920+. £120, $240.

355A

356. Note: There is no Figure 356 in this text.

Villeroy & Boch

Villeroy & Boch had and have factories in various countries in northwest Europe. Their output of spongeware has been extensive.

357. Bowl with beaded rim. 9″ diam. (23 cm). **GARDEN** all in blue. **Mark: the Wallerfangen mark in black with MADE IN THE SAAR BASIN and a stamped 13 38 W. See Mark no. 357A and KAD C85.** £70, $140.

357A

359. Plate. 9.1″ (23 cm). **VIRGINIA** with yellow stamens and purple sponged florets. **Mark: as above.** £80, $160.

358. Plate. 9.25″ (23.5 cm). Blue, sponge printed florets, painted large red and yellow flowers and foliage in two shades of green. **Mark: as above**. £60, $120.

360. Charger. 12.75″ (32.4 cm). **VIRGINIA** with a red rim line, yellow stamens and purple florets. The central motif has grown to meet the size of the piece. **Mark: as above.** £120, $240.

361. Serving dish. 9 x 7.5″ (22.9 x 19.1 cm). **VIRGINIA** with colors as above. **No mark.** £60, $120.

362. Plate. 11.625" (29.5 cm). **VIRGINIA** with a red rim line and purple sponged florets. A translation of the inscription reads: **TO BE CONTENT/A GREAT GOOD FORTUNE/TO REMAIN CONTENT/ A MASTERPIECE. Mark: as above**. £70, $140.

363. Plate. 6" (15.2 cm). **VIRGINIA** with a central green leaf. **Mark: VILLEROY & BOCH, WALLERFANGEN, MADE IN SAAR BASIN. See Mark no. 363A and KAD C85A.** £90, $180.

364. Soup plate. 8.125 x 1.875" (20.6 x 4.8 cm). The border has sponge printed blue flowers with red flares and yellow between green lines. The central flower is yellow with green foliage and blue sponge printed florets. **Mark: as above**. £90, $180.

365. Plate. 6.75" (17.1 cm). A blue rim line with stencilled foliage and sponge printed yellow flowers. **Mark: VILLEROY & BOCH, DRESDEN, SAXONY 5051**. £80, $160.

366. Bowl. 8.5" (21.6 cm). All in blue. Stencilled foliage and sponge printed flowers. **Mark: as above with 5053.** £60, $120.

367. Bowl. 11 x 5" (27.9 x 12.7 cm). Sponge printed yellow and blue flowers with red centers. The outside band has green leaves between the flowers. **Mark: the WALLERFANGEN mark**. **See Mark 367A.** £60, $120.

367A

367B

Note: later issue marked Made In Germany.

368. Plate. 9.25" (23.5 cm). Red lines enclose a band of blue sponge printing. The inner band mixes red and green motifs. **Mark: as above**. £60, $120.

369. Invalid's spit pot. Black lines and vertical sponge printed lines of motifs. Other motifs in blue and green. **Mark: as above**. Pieces of this type are often described as children's chamber pots but they are far too small for such use and their use as cuspidors for victims of tuberculosis seems more likely in view of the ubiquity of that disease during the era in question. £50, $100.

370. Bowl. 6.875 x 3" (17.5 x 7.6 cm). Black and green bands on either side of a broader band with overprinted black cross motifs. **Mark: as above**. £95, $190.

371. Bowl. 5.625 x 3.5" (14.3 x 8.9 cm). Red, green and blue lines and a brown band overprinted with black sponged motifs. **Mark: as above.** £90, $180.

372. Bowl. 4 x 1.5" (10.2 x 3.8 cm). Exterior decoration in red, green and blue sponge printed motifs. **Mark: VILLEROY & BOCH, DRESDEN, MADE IN GERMANY. See Mark 372A.** £80, $160.

372A

Italy

Italian spongeware does not seem ever to have been of very high quality. It is usually on a maiolica body and seems not to have been very popular.

373. Plate. 10" (25.4 cm). A blue sponge printed border and a painted scene with dabbed foliage in the maiolica tradition. There is a set of twelve of these with a plate for each month. **Mark: ITALY**. £75, $150.

374. Plate. 9.125" (23.2 cm). A blue sponged border, yellow flares, brown foliage and red sponged flowers. The central flower is blue and green. **Mark: a crown above three peaks and RICHARD GINORI, MORDOVI, ITALIA, FABRIQUE EN ITALIA, MADE IN ITALY. See Mark no. 374A.** £30, 60.

374A

375. Plate. 8.75" (22 cm). A blue sponge printed border. The center is painted in red and stencilled in green. **Mark: a green seal and circle with ITALIA, LSF, VINCENZA. See Mark no. 375A.** £90, $180.

375A

376. Soup plate. 8.75" (22 cm). All in blue. **Mark: illegible but for ITALIA**. £90, $180.

U.S.A.

Many manufacturers made spongeware in the U.S.A. but the preferred type of print seems to have been the indeterminate, loosely-textured sponge which looks early, though it never is in America. It is fully illustrated in McConnell.

377A

377-380. Plates and sherds, all from the Mayer Manufacturing Co./ Ardenal Pottery of Trenton. The mark partially seen on one sherd has a central shield with an M and the words **MAYER POTTERY M'fg CO**. The photographs were kindly provided by Mrs. Amy Earls. **See Mark no. 377A.** £50, $100 & £50, $100.

381. Bowl. c. 4″ diam (10.3 cm). Exterior decorated with a band of green floral motifs and gold spattering at the rim. The interior has a complicated green floral motif centrally and a little gold spattering at the rim. **Mark: COLUMBIAN ART POTTERY, TRENTON, N.J.** Collection: Hunterian Museum, University of Glasgow. £60, $120.

382. Plate. 8.5″ (21.6 cm). Blue sponge printed double diamonds over gold dabbing on the flange. **Mark: the Royal Arms with a central W and WARRANTED and W.M. CO. See Mark no. 382A.** £60, $120.

382A

383. Oval platter or ashet. 9.125 x 11.5″ (23.2 x 29.2 cm). A sponge printed border of purple flowers and brown leaves. **Mark: IVORY PORCELAIN BY SEBRING, REG. U.S. PATENT OFFICE 2-14-1925. SEBRING (OHIO). See Mark no. 383A.** £50, $100.

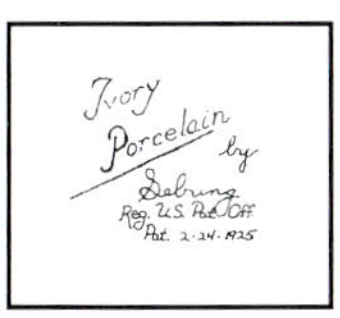

383A

384. Plate, 7.875″ (20 cm). A blue sponge printed border. **Mark: a lion facing out and unicorn flanking a crowned shield with an M. Above is IRONSTONE CHINA and below is MAYER POTTERY MFG. CO. MADE IN BEAVER FALLS, PA. See Mark 377A.** £70, $140.

385. Plate. 7.75" (19.7 cm). Two bands of sponge printing, the outer brown and the inner blue and brown. **Mark: as 381**. £60, $120.

386. Pudding plate. 7.75" (19.7 cm). Two bands of sponge printing, the outer green and the inner pink and green. Decorated in the interior. **See Mark no. 377A**. £80, $160.

387. Oval dish. 7.25 x 5.375 x 1.5" (18.4 x 13.7 x 3.8 cm). Sponge printed in blue. The border motif is repeated on the exterior. **See Mark no. 377A**. £40, $80.

388. Plate. 7.875" (20 cm). Blue sponge printed wreaths round brown flowers. **See Mark no. 377A.** £50, $100.

389. Pitcher or jug. 7 x 6" (17.8 x 15.2 cm). Sponge printed in green. Part of a ten piece bedroom set with the pattern name ARNO. It seems very small for a ewer. **Mark: WILLETS MANUFACTURING CO. of Trenton, N.J.** It is also known in blue. **See Mark no. 389A.** £50, $100.

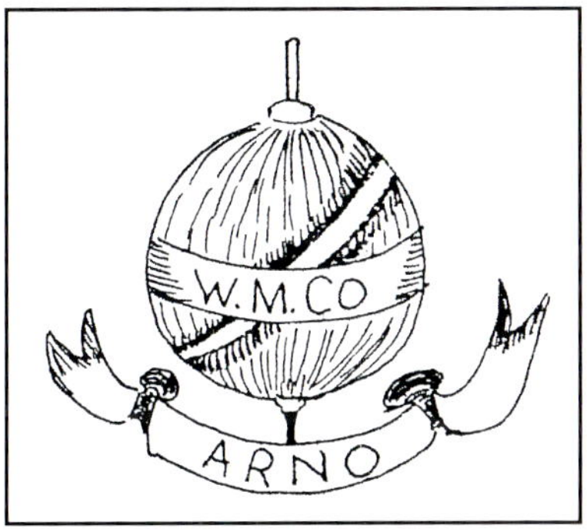

389A

390. Plate. 7" (17.8 cm). Blue sponge printing. **Mark: a roundel with two points and W. M. CO. across it . Below is a banner for ARNO. See Mark no. 389A.** £100, $200.

391. Sauceboat. 8.875 x 3.5" (22.4 x 8.9 cm). The Arno pattern as shown above, adjusted for shape. **See Mark 389A.** £100, $200.

392. Plate. Sponge printed in green. **Mark: MW in a shield for Morris Willmore CO., Trenton N.J. See Mark no. 392A.** £130, $260.

392A

394. Pitcher. As above. £110, $220.

393. Pitcher. c. 8″ (20.8 cm). All blue. The loosely-textured rather formless sponge printing favored by many American makers. **No mark** but of known American provenance. £50, $100.

Belgium

395. Soup plate. 11 x 2″ (27.9 x 5.1 cm). Blue lines and a red sponged border. Printed flowers and painted foliage and central flower. **Mark: MANUFACTURE IMPERIALE ET ROYALE FABRICATION BELGE MADE IN BELGIUM**. **See Mark no. 395A.** £90, $180.

395A

396. Bowl. 4.375″ (11.1 cm). Red lines, foliage and sponged flowers with blue flares. **Mark: as above.** £75, $150.

398. Plate. 8.625" (21.9 cm). A brown line and blue sponging on the border. The central spray is painted in black and green with red stenciled flowers. **The mark is illegible** but the plate was bought in Belgium. £70, $140.

397. Rice dish. 10.875 x 2.125" (27.6 x 5.4 cm). Blue lines enclose red and green sponged triangles. Painted yellow lines with red flares, green foliage and sponged blue flowers surround a central red and green flower. **Mark: as above but with NIMY** as place of manufacture. £100, $200.

400. Rice dish. 11" (27.9 cm). **GARDEN**. A black sponged border between red lines. Red flares, green foliage and blue sponged flowers. The central flower is red and green. **Mark: as 395A**. £50, $100.

399. Bowl. 8 x 3.5" (20.3 x 8.9 cm). The largest of a nesting set of six. A yellow rim line and a green line with red flares. Green foliage and blue sponged flowers. **Mark: as 394A**. £45, $90.

401. Bowl. 3.25" (8.3 cm). A red line and blue sponge printing with red sponged flowers and green foliage. **Mark: a shield flanked with B & F and MADE IN BELGIUM. See Mark no. 401A.** £50, $100.

401A

402. Plate. 8.75″ (22 cm). Red lines and painted green foliage. Sponge printed flowers in yellow with red centers and in blue. **Mark: MANUFACTURE IMPERIALE ET ROYALE FABRICATION BELGE NIMY MADE IN BELGIUM. See Mark no. 395A.** £65, $130.

403 and 404. Bowls. Both 4.5″ (11.4 cm). Both have broad red bands and green lines. In one the sponged motifs are red but the enclosing lines are yellow; in the other the lines are black. **Mark: a large circular figure with MADE IN BELGIUM around the top and BOCH FES LA LOUVIERE across the center. FABRICATION BELGE is around the bottom. See Mark no. 403A.** £50, $100 & £80, $160.

403A

405. Bowl. 5.5″ (14 cm). Black and red lines enclose a yellow band with sponged black motifs overpainted on it. **See Mark no. 395A.** £50, $100.

406. Saucer. 4″ (10.2 cm). Pairs of blue lines enclose a band of red sponge printing. A central band is sponged in green. **Mark: an impressed circle with BK and below MADE IN BELGIUM. See Mark no. 406A.** NP (No Price)

406A

Ireland

We must assume that the only pottery to make spongeware until recent years in Ireland was Belleek. This is sometimes marked but more often not. It seems to be distinguished by a grayish green body and usually by two motifs alternating either in one row or in two staggered rows.

407. Mug. 4.25" (10.8 cm). Two rounds of sponge printing, green above and red below. **Mark: the later Belleek mark. See Mark no. 407A.** £60, $120.

407A

408. Mug. 4" (10.2 cm). Two rows of sponge printing, brown above and red below. **Mark: as above**. 407 and 408 both agree with the description of Belleek wares given above. £80, $160.

409. Belleek mark on both 407 and 408.

410. Mug. c. 4" (10.2 cm). A band of alternating crimson "berries" and blue flowers round the rim. The body and the type of decoration would indicate this as a product of Belleek Pottery although there is **No mark.** Collection: Hunterian Museum, University of Glasgow. £300, $600.

Russia

So far all that is known of Russian manufacture is the name Kuznietsoff impressed on pieces, mostly to be found in the U.S.A. The script used is Cyrillic and pre-revolutionary, giving a date before 1918. It seems likely that many of them arrived in the U.S.A. in the luggage of immigrants. Many of them are decorated in a mixture of sponge printing and brushstroke in a subdued range of colors. Some are illustrated in Greaser.

411 and 412. Soup plate. Decorated with a violet/gray stripe at the rim with a black sponged motif. On the floor of the plate are three painted flowers in yellow and dark orange with black stems and pale green foliage with three tiny sponged blue flowers. **Mark: impressed and printed in black both, it has the imperial eagle and Kuznietsoff on a ribbon with other words in unclear script. See Mark no. 411A.** £300, $600.

411A

"Irish Potato Bowls"

The name is one of convenience since almost certainly none of them is of Irish manufacture, although they are found most frequently in Ireland. Most probably they are principally Scottish in origin but some may well be English. They can be easily confused with the washbowl from a bedroom set, particularly when they occur singly and alone and they are not necessarily different from them in any significant way. It may be that only their history is different. But they can be seen in Irish collections in sets of two or three which would militate against their being meant for a bedroom. No marked specimens have ever been reported.

413. Bowl with everted rim. c. 12" (30.5 cm). The rim and the floor have each a band of light blue motifs. Between is a band of two alternate complex motifs. One is of a pale puce feather overprinted with green "daisies;" the other is a complex sponge of a basket of flowers in the three colors already mentioned. This last is repeated in the center of the floor. This would have been relatively time consuming in the making and consequently fairly expensive. **No mark.** Collection: Hunterian Museum, University of Glasgow. £300, $600.

414. Potato bowl with everted rim and dimensions similar to 413. The structure of the decoration is similar to 413 except that there are four black lines separating the various bands. On this bowl the two simple, sponge printed bands are an identical floral motif. Between and on the floor of the bowl is a motif in crimson and black of two flowers on a twig. **No mark.** Collection: Kingussie, Highland Folk Museum, Highland Council. £275, $550.

415. Bowl with everted rim and similar dimensions to 413. All decoration in brown. Double lines enclose two "chain" bands and between these is a band of floral motifs, one of which appears again in the center of the floor. **No mark.** Collection: Ulster Folk and Transport Museum, NMGNI. £250, $500.

416. Bowl with everted rim and dimensions similar to 413. Four brown lines enclose various bands. The first and third rows are in blue and floral, the second row is of shaded brown sycamore leaves, one of which also appears in the center of the floor. **No mark.** Collection: Ulster Folk and Transport Museum, NMGNI. NP

417. Bowl with everted rim and similar dimension to 413. There are five motifs, three of which are in bands. The rim has a brown motif of foliage which is repeated as band three. The second band has brown fans with blue leaves attached; the fourth band has a different shape of fan with double blue leaves. In the center of the floor is a motif of flowers and leaves in brown and blue. **No mark.** Collection: Ulster Folk and Transport Museum, NMGNI. £400, $800.

418 and 419. 13.5" (34.3 cm). All decoration is in brown. The six birds each have a worm. There is a motif on the outside. **No mark.** £250, $500 & £90, $180.

Southeast Asian Exports

The picture of wares exported to southeast Asia is one that is unfolding before our eyes; it is certainly not even approximately complete yet. The first hints came from sherds with Bells' mark found all over central Glasgow during the widespread demolition of tenement buildings from the 1950s to the 1970s. Many of these showed very Oriental transfer patterns which agreed with Fleming's statement that Bells had employed Chinese designers. Then Edwin Robertson brought hundreds of plates and rice dishes back from Indonesia bearing these patterns and others were subsequently identified from Myanmar and Malaysia.

Since then, many spongeware dishes have been found from India to Sarawak, including a large collection from Sri Lanka. This time, however, Bells is not by any means the only manufacturer involved nor Scotland the only country. Besides them, we have from Scotland Methven (Links Pottery), Cochran (Verreville and Britannia Potteries) and McNay (Bridgeness Pottery); from England Adams and George Jones, both of whom were also prolific exporters to the U.S.A.; from Holland Petrus Regout (Sphinx Pottery) and the Société Cêramique. There are even rather odd pieces from Japan whose potteries must have learned very quickly from the others.

The pieces are mostly soup plate or rice dishes but there are some dinner plates. Pitchers seem to be unknown in spongeware and uncommon in any other form of decoration. What is remarkable about these pieces is their size; normal for the rice dish is about 10 inches but there are pieces which are more than 15 inches in diameter. These must have been difficult to pot and fire successfully. The standard of decoration, too, is much higher than in the normal run of spongeware. It is clear that this market was not considered as demeaning as the more normal market.

The trade must have flourished from the 1880s until the First World War. It is possible that some of the potteries carried on longer than this. That both the Bells' transfer prints and the spongeware pieces were immensely popular is evident both from the numbers that still exist and the honor in which certain pieces are held by their present owners. This is beautifully illustrated by two pages of photographs in Myanmar Style. They are now eagerly collected on at least four continents. Nos. 528-533 are part of a series brought back from India and now scattered in private collections. They seem to belong stylistically to an earlier era than most export ware from this part of the world so far known. It seems quite likely that the Indian market was opened up before the rest of southeast Asia.

The Durrie collection contained a hint of the limits of our knowledge in that one obvious export piece is labeled as having been bought in Persia (Iran). This is an area that is still totally unexplored.

The preponderance of Methven pieces among the Scottish wares probably reflects their care with marking rather than their share of the market, which was nevertheless obviously quite large.

420. Large bowl. 13.1" (33.5 cm). Four crimson lines on interior. Between one and two is a band of purple sponge printed motifs; between two and three painted crimson flares, blue flowers and green leaves. Between four and a thick crimson band are blue buds and crimson, green and blue foliage. In any other context and with different decoration this would be considered an "Irish Potato Bowl." **Mark: an impressed B in a bell. From India.** £130, $260.

421. Rice dish. Four crimson lines. Between one and two is a band of sponge printed crimson flowers. Between three and four a band of abstract green motifs. Between four and a thick crimson line are four blue fleur-de-lis-like motifs alternating with radiating lines in crimson of an abstract motif. **Mark: an impressed B in a bell**. An exactly similar piece is illustrated in Cruickshank as being in Scotland. From India. **See KAD B222.** £200, $400.

422. Rice dish. **GARDEN** in black, blue, brown and crimson. Found quite often in Scotland but bearing a **mark for the firm of S. Oppenheimer & Co. Ltd**. of Rangoon. Sherds with this pattern and mark have been found on a Bells' sherd dump. £150, $300.

423. Rice dish. 11" diam. (28 cm). The three plum pattern was made by several of the exporting potteries. It is obvious that they copied each other's patterns. **Mark: impressed B in a bell**. From Sri Lanka. **See KAD B222.** £250, $500.

424. Rice dish. 10" diam. (25.4 cm). Wholly sponge printed. A blue arched motif at the edge, then a small red leaf motif in a band. Centrally there is a red "peony" with green leaves. **Mark: impressed B in a bell**. From Sri Lanka. £200, $400.

457. Rice dish. 12.375" (31.5 cm). All in crimson, eight lines. Between 2 and 3, 4 and 5, 6 and 7, there are double bands of checks. A central "aster." **Mark: impressed George Jones mark and stamped oval mark**. From Sri Lanka. £100, $200.

458. Rice dish. 14.5'' (37 cm). **PERSIAN ROSE** with black foliage and yellow sponge printed dots. A central "rose" in crimson, green and black. **Mark: impressed George Jones mark with an omega and NVS in red.** From Sri Lanka. £180, $360.

459. Rice dish. 14.75" (13.5 cm). Blue "asters" joined by a black line with green leaves and outlined crimson flowers. A central blue "aster." **Mark: oval with STAFFORDSHIRE, ENGLAND**, probably for **George Jones**. From Sri Lanka. £150, $300.

460. Rice dish. 14.625" (37 cm). A crimson rim line encloses a band of decoration very like that above but that the flowers are blue and smaller. The central element is made up of six painted leaves and a crimson flower. **Mark: ADAMS with stag. See KAD B28.** From Sri Lanka. £200, $400.

461. Rice dish. 14.5″ (37 cm). A totally painted design. Two crimson lines enclose a large crimson flower with purple sepals and green leaves and three smaller crimson flowers. **Mark as above**. From Sri Lanka. £180, $360.

462. Rice dish. 12″ (30.5 cm). All in blue. A lattice motif with trefoil hangs from a blue line at the rim. Two other lines enclose a band of leaf motifs and there is a central floral group. **Mark: as above (without England), c. 1879-1890**. From Sri Lanka. £200, $400.

463. Soup plate. 8.25″ (21 cm). All flow blue. Four lines. Between 1 and 2 a band of abstract motifs, repeated between 2 and 3. **Mark: as above**. From Sri Lanka. £200, $400.

464. Rice dish. 8.5″ (21.5 cm). All blue with three lines. Between 1 and 2, a lattice motif. Between 2 and 3, groups of three leaves. Centrally, four abstract motifs. **Mark: as no. 462.** From Sri Lanka. £150, $300.

465. Rice dish. 14.75" (37.5 cm). The three plums pattern with a blue floral border. This pattern was much used by Adams. **Mark: as no. 462**. From Sri Lanka. £95, $190.

466. Rice dish. 12" (30.5 cm). The three plum pattern, this time with no border motif at all. **Mark: Adams with stag and ENGLAND**. **See KAD B28.** From Sri Lanka. £180, $360.

467. Rice dish. 8.75" (22 cm). Dark border with purple grapes and green leaves. . **Mark: Adams with stag and ENGLAND**. **See KAD B28.** From Sri Lanka. £150, $300.

468. Rice dish. 11.75" (30 cm). Three crimson "asters" with green leaves and blue sponge printed florets. A central crimson bud with green leaves. . **Mark: Adams with stag and ENGLAND**. **See KAD B28.** From Sri Lanka. £100, $200.

469. Rice dish. 10.75" (27.5 cm.) As 464 but with groups of four leaves instead of three. **Mark: Adams with stag and ENGLAND**. **See KAD B28.** From Sri Lanka. £90, $180.

470. Rice dish. 14.625" (37 cm). Three yellow lines. Yellow "flares" hang from the first and blue daisies with green leaves grow from the second. A central "aster" in green and blue. **Mark: Adams with stag and ENGLAND**. **See KAD B28.** From Sri Lanka. £80, $160.

471. Rice dish. 14.5" (37 cm). Much the same pattern as 456 with different sponge printed flowers. **Mark: STAFFORDSHIRE, ENGLAND**. From Sri Lanka. £90, $180.

472. Rice dish. 14.5" (37 cm). Much the same pattern as the above but with yellow outer "asters" and foliage. **Mark: STAFFORDSHIRE, ENGLAND**. From Sri Lanka. £160, $320.

473. Rice dish. 10.5" (26.5 cm). The same pattern as 472 but all the "asters" are red and the sponged flowers are blue. **Mark: BAKER & CO. Ltd. ENGLAND, OLD ENGLISH HAND-PAINTED. See Mark no. 203A.** From Sri Lanka. £200, $400.

474. Rice dish. 8.5" (21.5 cm). **PERSIAN ROSE** with solid flowers and a central yellow "aster" and without any sponge printing. This looks like the work of a pottery that came late on the scene and had not quite understood the patterns made by the others. **Mark: CHURCH GRESLEY. See Mark no. 240A.** From Sri Lanka. £60, $120.

475. Soup plate. 10.625" (27 cm). Two black lines. A rim band of crimson flowers with green leaves. **Mark: impressed LONDON and an anchor.** From Sri Lanka. £70, $140.

476. Soup plate. 9" (22.25 cm). Four blue lines. Between 1 and 2, a band of two blue motifs. Between 3 and 4, radial red stripes with yellow sponged motifs alternate with blue and green leaves and black curved lines. **Mark: lions**. From Sri Lanka. £70, $140.

477. Bowl. 5.75″ (15 cm). Two green lines enclose a wide brown stripe. A third green line and then a black line with crimson flowers, green leaves and blue dots**. Mark: MADE IN ENGLAND in a rectangle.** From Sri Lanka. £120, $240.

478. Rice dish. 8.25″ (21 cm). As 477 with a central element. **Mark: as above**. From Sri Lanka. £80, $160.

479. Rice dish. 8.25″ (21 cm). Three red "aster" pattern again. **Same mark as 447**. From Sri Lanka. £80, $160.

480. Rice dish. 11″ (28 cm). **GARDEN** in black, yellow, crimson, blue and brown. **Mark: MADE IN ENGLAND**. From Sri Lanka. £60, $120.

481 and 482. Bowl. 3.25" (8.25 cm). Iron lustre on rim and flares; red printed dot flowers and green foliage. The interior has a crimson star and crescent. The motif of the crescent is uncommon and seems to be confined to the Dutch potteries and to Moslem countries. **Mark: Petrus Regout**. From Sri Lanka. £210, $420.

483. Two bowls. Both 3.25" (8.25 cm). One with crude **PERSIAN ROSE** and the other with red "asters." **Mark: Petrus Regout**. From Sri Lanka. £120, $240.

484. Rice dish. 11" (28 cm). The three red "asters" pattern with a painted blue element. Centrally there are a crescent and star in crimson. **Mark: Petrus Regout**. From Sri Lanka. £250, $500.

485. Rice dish. 10.25" (26 cm). **PERSIAN ROSE** with blue and red roses. Crimson and yellow circles centrally, enclosing a blue and red painted flower with green leaves. **Mark: Petrus Regout**. From Sri Lanka. £130, $260.

486. Rice dish. 9.5″ (24.25 cm). **GARDEN** in black, yellow, crimson, blue and brown. **Mark: Petrus Regout**. From Sri Lanka. £60, $120.

487. Rice dish. 12.5″ (31.75 cm). A black sponge printed rim between crimson lines. The central area has three plumlike fruits on a black stem with green leaves and blue flowers. Very elegant. **Mark: Petrus Regout.** From Sri Lanka. £80, $160.

488. Rice dish. 10.75″ (27 cm). A crimson line. Three crimson flowers joined by black lines with green leaves and blue dot flowers. Central crimson buds with green leaves. **Mark: Petrus Regout and a foreign script.** From Sri Lanka. £130, $260.

489. Bowl. 7.125″ (20 cm). Four green lines: 1 and 2 enclose a wide brown band; between 3 and 4, a black line carries crimson flowers, green leaves and blue dots. **Mark: Société Cêramique.** From Sri Lanka. £130, $260.

490. Rice dish. 14.25″ (36 cm). The same as 489 but with a central "aster." **Mark: as above**. From Sri Lanka. £140, $280.

491, 492, 493, 494. A bowl and 3 rice dishes. 7.5" (18.5 cm), 10.5" (26.5 cm), 9.5" (24.25 cm), 14" (35.5 cm). Variations on the three plum pattern. **Marks: all Société Cêramique**. From Sri Lanka. £140, $280; £100, $200; £110, $220; & £110, $220.

495, 496, 497, 498, 499. Rice dishes. 14.375" (36.5 cm), 8.5" (21.5 cm), 14.5" (36 cm), 13.25" (33.5 cm). Variations on **GARDEN**. **All Société Cêramique**. From Sri Lanka. £100, $200; £95, $190; £150, $300; £150, $300; & £110, $220.

500, 501, 502. Rice dishes. 14.375" (36.5 cm), 14.5" (36.625 cm), 12.375" (31.5 cm). Five-Petal pattern. **Mark: Société Cêramique**. From Sri Lanka. £200, $400; £100, $200; & £80, $160.

503. Rice dish. 14.25" (36 cm). **PERSIAN ROSE** with blue and red roses and a central crescent and star in yellow. **Same as mark 489**. From Sri Lanka. £110, $220.

504. Rice dish. 13.5" (34 cm). A very distorted **VIRGINIA** with a central crimson flower **Same as mark 489**. From Sri Lanka. £170, $340.

505. Rice dish. 10.5" (26.75 cm). The same pattern as 482 with a slightly varied central element. **Same as mark 489**. From Sri Lanka. £120, $240.

506. Rice dish. 13" (33 cm). A crimson line inside which is an edge band of several elements: (a) four crimson flowers with six green leaves printed; (b) seven painted green leaves with a black zigzag; (c) six printed blue stars. Each has four repeats. **Same as mark 489**. From Sri Lanka. £120, $240.

507. Rice dish. 8.5" (21.5 cm). A central crimson "aster" with blue printed flowers and dark green leaves, lighter leaves are painted. Two crimson lines. **Same as mark 489**. From Sri Lanka. £120, $240.

508. Rice dish. 13.5" (31.25 cm). A central crimson "aster" with black "stalks" bearing green leaves and buds and flowers in blue. A crimson rim line. **Mark: as 489**. From Sri Lanka. £100, $200.

509. Rice dish. 8.25" (21 cm). Central crimson "aster" and the same border groups as number 506. **Same as mark 489**. From Sri Lanka. £60, $120.

510. Rice dish. 14.5" (36 cm). Central crimson "aster" grows on a black "stalk" and has green painted and printed leaves and blue printed flowers. **Same as mark 489**. From Sri Lanka. £90, $180.

511. Rice dish. 12.25" (31 cm). Central green and blue "aster." Three yellow lines. 1 and 2 enclose blue "flares" and groups of three blue daisies with green leaves. **Same as mark 489**. From Sri Lanka. £210, $420.

514A

512. Bowl. 7.75" (19.5 cm). **PERSIAN ROSE** with solid flowers. **Same as mark 489**. From Sri Lanka. £90, $180.

513. Rice dish. 8.25" (20 cm). Five black lines. 1 and 2 enclose a wide yellow band with black overprinted motifs. Between 2 and 3 red and green stripes. **Same as mark 489**. From Sri Lanka. £90, $180.

514. Rice dish. 9.75" (25.5 cm). A crimson line edges a broad blue band with negative crescent and star motifs. A blue line and then a black line bears pink flowers and green leaves with blue dots. Two black lines edge a central solid blue area with a negative star. **Mark: green transfer. A shield with KNAZW and "rays," flanked by two fantasy birds and foliage. Above is IMPERIAL IRONSTONE CHINA; below is NIPPONKOSHITSUTOLICO. and MADE IN JAPAN. See Mark no. 514A.** From Sri Lanka. £95, $190.

515. Rice dish. 8.625" (22 cm). Two crimson lines enclose a travesty of **VIRGINIA**. Centrally, green leaves and a crimson stem bear three repeats of the blue sponged motifs from the border. **No mark** but there is a close resemblance to the next entry. From Sri Lanka. £150, $300.

516. Rice dish. 8.5" (21.5 cm). Almost identical to 515. **Mark: an outlined regal crown** in the same color of transfer as number 514; the body and the crazed glaze are also similar so it is thought that this mark belongs to the same Company as 514. From Sri Lanka. £180, $360.

517. Rice dish. 8.5" (21.5 cm). The Three "Aster" pattern with both blue and brown sponge printing. **Mark: same as above**. From Sri Lanka. £95, $190.

518. Soup plate. 8.75" (22 cm). Crimson line and border of sponged flowers. The center has a stencilled vase and painted crimson flowers with green leaves. **Mark: Sarreguemines**. From Sri Lanka. £110, $220.

519. Soup plate. 7.875" (20 cm). Crimson line. Overall a black stem with green and crimson leaves and floral elements in crimson, blue, yellow and orange. There is no sponged element**. Mark: Sarreguemines**. From Sri Lanka. £120, $240.

520. Rice dish. 8.75" (22 cm). "Scottish flow blue." A central blue "aster" and a rim of doubled sponge printed elements. **Mark: the PETTAH**. Origin unknown. From Sri Lanka. £200, $400.

521. Bowl. 6.25" (16 cm). "Scottish flow blue." Two-tier printed patterns inside and outside. **Mark: the PETTAH**. Origin unknown. From Sri Lanka. £200, $400.

522. Rice dish. 13.25" (33.5 cm). Three crimson lines enclose a yellow band with black overprints. Groups of three sponged crimson flowers with green foliage depend from the third line. A fourth crimson line. **Mark: PRIMAVESI & SON, CARDIFF. Same as mark 246A.** Origin unknown. From Sri Lanka. £90, $180.

523. Rice dish. 12.375" (31.6 cm). Rim line crimson as are the small paired leaves. The sponged florets are blue and the rest is green. **No mark.** From Iran. NP

524. Rice dish. Three crimson asters with green foliage and blue sepals. Central crescent and star in crimson. **No mark.** From Bali. £110, $220.

525. Rice dish. Crimson lines and flowers with green leaves, a black line joining them and sponge printed dots. From Bali. **See next entry.** £120, $240.

525A. Mark on the rice dish portrayed in no. 525.

527. Plate. A variant of **GARDEN** in very rich colors. **No mark.** From Bali. £140, $280.

528. Bowl with beaded, everted rim. Between two crimson lines a band of crimson, floral motifs, then a band of blue daisies. Centrally there is a crimson "peony" with green leaves. **No mark but the shape and the type would seem to indicate Methven of Kirkcaldy**. From India. £300, $600.

529. Bowl. Three flow blue lines. Between 1 and 2 there is a band of floral motifs in the same colour. **No mark.** From India. £120, $240.

530. Soup plate. c. 8″ (20.5 cm). All in blue. Three blue lines separating three bands of different motifs. **No mark.** From India. £110, $220.

531. Baking dish. The rim has a band of crimson motifs and the well is covered with a lacustrine landscape in crimson transfer print. This is a relatively early type of ware and should date at the latest from the middle of the nineteenth century. **No mark.** From India. £70, $140.

532. Soup plate. c. 8″ (20.5 cm). The decoration consists entirely of crimson lines and two bands of an abstract motif in green. **No mark.** From India. £90, $180.

533. Soup plate. c. 8″ (20.5 cm). All in blue. The rim has a floral motif in blue. In the well swags of daisies have printed flowers inside the swags and brushed leaves outside. **No mark.** From India. £80, $160.

Portugal

There seems to have been some manufacture of spongeware in Portugal, though the date and place is uncertain.

534. Plate. c. 7" (17.8 cm). Pink and yellow flowers with green and brown foliage and a touch of blue occupy the well of the plate surrounded by two black lines. The edge has a sponged triangular pattern. **No mark.** £100, $200.

Nonattributed, Miscellaneous

The vastly major proportion of spongeware, no matter what its origin, is unmarked and practically unattributable, certainly so in the present state of our knowledge. Wholly printed pieces and pieces with sponge printing combined with brushstroke work, even pieces composed solely of hand-painting can all come from the same source; so, dividing the pieces up in that way is not helpful. In the past dividing the pieces up into types of pattern has been found mildly helpful with attributions but not spectacularly so. In a world where potters were very mobile and where commercial firms supplied ready-made sponges to potteries, it is impossible to attribute pieces on the strength of one motif, or even on the coincidence of several unless the several form a very distinctive pattern.

Since overwhelmingly the Durrie collection of photographs consisted of unmarked, fairly ordinary spongeware and since this coincides with what one meets in everyday life, it seems impossible to treat this section with the rigid order which one would like to apply. The selection of headings and divisions is based solely on what seemed most useful, given the pieces that are at our disposal in writing this work.

"Careful Dabbing"

This type of pattern is defined by a band of dabbing round the rim of the piece. Overlapping this there is a band of sponge printing, usually of flowers or birds. These pieces are seldom marked though one has been reported stamped MADE IN ENGLAND and one is shown here with a mark perhaps for George Jones.

535. Bowl. 6.25 x 3" (15.9 x 7.6 cm). An internal brown line. A sponge print of red and yellow flowers and green leaves over brown dabbing. **Mark: Royal Arms and STAFFORDSHIRE**. £140, $280.

536. Bowl. c. 4" (10.2 cm). Dabbed in purplish blue with a band of crimson and green floral motifs. The rhythmic marks of the dabbing are clearly visible. **No mark.** Collection: Hunterian Museum, University of Glasgow. £70, $140.

537. Mug. c. 4" (10.2 cm). Dabbing in red and sponge printing in blue, green and yellow floral motifs. **No mark.** £70, $140.

538. Bowl. c. 6" (15.2 cm). Dabbing in blue with a band of complex motifs of birds alternating with floral motifs; black, brown, yellow, crimson and green are all present. **No mark.** Collection: Hunterian Museum, University of Glasgow. £70, $140.

539. Mug. 4" (10.2 cm). Dabbing in yellow with sponge printed blue flowers and green foliage. **No mark.** £150, $300.

540. Bowl. 6.375" (16.2 cm). Dabbing in blue with sponge printing in blue also. **Mark: rampant horses flank an oval with STAFFORDSHIRE, ENGLAND.** £120, $240. **See mark 271A.**

541. Bowl. 5" (12.7 cm). Dabbing in red with blue and green sponge printed motifs. **No mark.** £160, $320.

Rabbits

This is a very peculiar series of plates combining very anthropomorphic transfer prints of rabbits with painted and printed floral motifs. They have never been reported from Britain and would seem to be a product intended for the U.S. market. As such, it is most likely that their manufacturer was a U.S. or an English firm, even a Staffordshire firm. The date must be late in the sequence and 1930 would not appear to be too late.

542. Mug. 5.75" (14.6 cm). **VIRGINIA** in central band. The top and bottom bands have red lines and brown transfers of rabbits with painted green frogs and foliage. **No mark.** £120, $240.

543. Mug. 5.5" (14 cm). Blue sponge printed flowers and green florets, painted red buds, green and blue foliage. Brown transfer of rabbits overwashed in yellow, apart from rabbits and a large green painted frog. Red lines. **No mark.** £160, $320.

544. Plate. 9.25" (23.5 cm). **VIRGINIA** with red, blue and yellow flowers and blue sponged flowers. Transfer print of rabbits playing tennis. **Registration number for 1905**. £160, $320.

545. Plate. 9" (22.9 cm). Blue and red sponge printed florets with **VIRGINIA** type flowers and sponged blue flowers. Painted red flowers and lines. Four gray transfer prints of rabbits. **No mark.** £140, $280.

546 & 547. Plates. 9.25" (23.5 cm). Large brown prints of rabbits painted green and yellow. The edges have blue sponge printed and red painted flowers with green foliage. **Registration mark for 1905**. £120, $240 & £160, $320.

548. Plate. 9" (22.9 cm). Brown rabbit prints with yellow wash. Sponge printed blue flowers and large red painted flowers with green foliage. Red rim line. **No mark.** £150, $300.

549. Plate. 9.25" (23.5 cm). Brown rabbit print round the rim with yellow wash and green frogs and cabbage. The second band has painted and sponge printed elements. The innermost band is blue and the central florets are red round a single blue one. **No mark.** £150, $300.

550. Platter or ashet. 15 x 10.75" (38.1 x 27.3 cm). The rim has the same decoration as the previous piece's middle band. Inside is a brown rabbit print with a yellow wash. **No mark.** £120, $240.

551. Plate. 9" (22.9 cm). Brown rabbit print with yellow wash. **VIRGINIA** border with blue sponge printed florets. **No mark.** £120, $240.

552. Plate. 9.25" (23.5 cm). A brown rabbit print with a yellow wash. **Outer band as 549**. **No mark.** £50, $100.

553. Plate. 9.25" (23.5 cm). Outer band is brown rabbit print. Center is **VIRGINIA**. **No mark**. £60, $120.

554. Plate. 7" (17.8 cm). Rabbit print on outer band; middle band is **PERSIAN ROSE** with no sponge printing; the central sponge printed flowers are red and blue. **No mark.** £70, $140.

Bows and Swags

Almost always blue bows and green swags. This pattern is found almost exclusively on bowls and mugs. It is so classic that it has been labeled by one researcher "the Bo'ness bow" and this could be correct but is by no means certain. Only one specimen occurred in the Durrie collection and the distribution otherwise would certainly suggest a Scottish origin.

556. Mug. c. 4" (10.2 cm). The swags here have become leaf motifs. **No mark.** £80, $160.

555. Mug. c. 4.5" (11.4 cm). This is the classic form which can be found all over Scotland, Ireland and Canada. **No mark.** £90, $180.

557 Plate. 7.5" (19.1 cm). Red bows are connected by green swags. An example is shown by Finlayson with **GUID MORNING** in the center, giving an almost certain Scottish origin. £120, $240.

Early Looking Pieces

These are characterized by rather shapeless but still repetitive patterns such as are found on the earliest sherds excavated from sites such as Bo'ness Pottery. There is, of course, no guarantee that such pieces, found whole, are necessarily early (i.e. c. 1840), especially since such patterns seem to have remained popular with some American potteries until quite a late period. There is a tendency too to confuse such patterns with purely dabbed ware but very often the motif on the sponge can be seen on close examination.

558. Bowl. c. 6" (15.2 cm). A blue motif mingles with a faint crimson motif. **No mark.** Collection: Hunterian Museum, University of Glasgow. £110, $220.

559. Bowl. Three motifs, each in a different color, are superimposed on each other between black lines. **No mark.** Collection: Hunterian Museum, University of Glasgow. £90, $180.

560. Pitcher. 8.5" high (21.6 cm). Blue lines and vague blue motifs. **No mark.** £60, $120.

561. Mug. c. 6.5″ (16.5 cm). Blue painted bands enclose a vague pattern of sponge print in a deeper blue. **No mark.** £120, $240.

562. Plate c. 8″ (20.3 cm). A painted four-petaled flower with blue and green elements is central while the flange is covered in a sponged motif of indeterminate cut. **No mark.** Collection: Hunterian Museum, University of Glasgow. £120, $240.

563. Plate. c. 8″ (20.3 cm). The flange is covered with indeterminate brown motifs, one of which dips into the body of the plate. Centrally there is another floral motif. **No mark.** Collection: Hunterian Museum, University of Glasgow. £60, $120.

564. Ewer. c. 9.5″ (24.1 cm). All in blue. Six lines in pairs and four bands of sponge printing. Each seem to be emerging from formlessness into floral shapes. **No mark.** £80, $160.

565. Mug. c. 5″ (12.7 cm). Vertical stripes in sepia and blue are the only decoration. These are certainly dabbed rather than sponge printed. Collection: Kingussie, the Highland Folk Museum, Highland Council, Scotland. **No mark.** £70, $140.

Cable Borders

These are attributed by Finlayson to Annfield Pottery but in fact they were used by a great variety of potteries in Scotland and England.

566. Plate. 7.75" (19.7 cm). A cable border in purple. The inner band has red flowers and green leaves. **No mark.** £70, $140.

567. Bowl. c. 8" (20.3 cm). Cable borders in blue at rim and base. Between are repetitions of a two-colored, floral motif in crimson and green. **No mark.** Almost certainly Scottish, perhaps Methven. £90, $180.

568. Bowl. 6.75" (17.1 cm). A cable band in green, then red flowers and green leaves. **No mark.** £90, $180.

Double Diamond

This is a very miscellaneous group which undoubtedly has a variety of origins; so the double diamond can take many different forms.

569. Bowl. 5.375 x 3.5″ (13.7 x 8.9 cm). Sponge printed in blue with double diamonds. **Unmarked.** £100, $200.

570. Bowl. c. 6″ (15.2 cm). A band of double diamonds in blue hovers over two-colored daisy motifs in crimson and green. **No mark.** Collection: Hunterian Museum, Glasgow University. £160, $320.

571. Bowl. c. 4.5″ (11.1 cm). Double diamonds in purple under a zigzag of the same color. Below is a band of green foliage motifs. **No mark.** £110, $220.

572. Chamber pot. c. 8.5″ (21.6 cm). A simple double diamond in green is the only decoration. It occurs on the everted rim, on the belly of the pot and on the handle. **No mark.** Collection: Hunterian Museum, University of Glasgow. £150, $300.

573. Rice dish. c. 9″ (22.9 cm). Five black lines enclose four bands of double diamonds in a slightly flown blue. **No mark.** £70, $140.

574. Invalid spit pot. c. 4″ (10.2 cm). A band of large blue double diamonds covers the belly of the pot and has superimposed brown "stars." **No mark.** £110, $220.

575. Pitcher. c. 8″ (20.3 cm). A network of double diamonds in dark green encloses pale pink motifs with green leaves. **No mark.** Collection: Ulster Folk and Transport Museum, NMGNI. £120, $240.

576. Mug. 3.25″ (8.3 cm). Red lines and green sponge printed double diamonds. **No mark.** £100, $200.

577. Plate. 9″ (22.9 cm). Red lines with green double diamonds and part circles in red. **No mark.** £100, $200.

Twigged Flowers & Blue Lines

This is a very clearly defined group. The decoration consists of four elements: crimson flowers, green leaves, brown twigs (all sponge printed), and painted blue lines. The only variants seem to be the crimson flowers and the number of blue lines. No marked example has so far been found. On the strength of the "Glasgow Rose," which is the most commonly seen of the flowers and is clearly based on C. R. Mackintosh's designs, the date can be given as c. 1900. At that date there are few Glasgow potteries which could have made it and Kirkcaldy seems also to be a possible source.

578. Two bowls. c. 8" (20.3 cm). These show all the elements mentioned above and display the "Glasgow Rose." **No mark.** Collections: Hunterian Museum, Glasgow University and private collection. £100, $200.

579. Bowl. c. 6" (15.2 cm). This one shows a daisy in place of the rose. Collection: Hunterian Museum, Glasgow University. **No mark.** £110, $220.

580. Bowl. c. 6" (15.2 cm). Only one blue line and a different flower. Otherwise, this bowl decoration very similar to both the above entries in 578 and 579. Flowers of this type have been found on sherds dating from the correct period and from Britannia Pottery. **No mark.** £110, $220.

581. Bowl with beaded rim. 9.25" (23.5 cm). Three yellow lines. The first two enclose a band of black heart shapes, the second and third enclose seven "Glasgow Roses" joined by green foliage and double blue swags. **No mark.** This is rather different from the others in this group but seems to have enough points of similarity to be included. £100, $200.

Hard Edge or Camellia Pattern

The latter name is used by Durrie, who claims it is used by collectors. The essential elements are groups of green leaves and of red or purple flowers in varying numbers and arrangements. These are combined with painted lines. What gives the group stylistic coherence is the extremely clean cut of the sponges which look almost like stencilled decoration. No 186 should rightfully belong here and bears an ADAMS mark. Certainly something very similar is illustrated in Furniss & Wagner. In any case, the group is certainly English in origin.

582. Plate. 8.75" (22 cm). Green leaves and purple flowers. **No mark.** £100, $200.

583. Soup plate. 8.75" (22 cm). Red flowers and five clusters of leaves but no centerpiece. **No mark.** £100, $200.

584. Cup and saucer. Red line with blue sponge printed flowers and green leaves. **No mark.** £130, $260.

585. Cup and saucer. **No mark.** £70, $140.

586. Plate. Blue flowers and red leaves. **No mark.** £140, $280.

587. Rice dish. 10.75" (27.3 cm). Decoration on concave. Lines and leaves are green, border flowers red and inner bands purple. **No mark.** £90, $180.

588. Saucer. Blue floral border and central flowers in red with leaves in two shades of green. **No mark.** £90, $180.

Totally Miscellaneous

At this point the attempt to codify the vast mass of spongeware must be given up and what follows is a rich array of the commoner (and some less common), unmarked types of spongeware which may well remain a mystery for all time but nevertheless give great pleasure to collectors and users both.

589. Bowl. Rim and base have bands of blue floral motifs. The belly of the bowl has a row of crimson "raspberries" with green leaves in two separate sponges. **No mark.** £90, $180.

591. Mug. 3.25" (8.3 cm). Purple lines with green, pink and yellow sponge prints. **No mark**. £80, $160.

590. Plate. A rim pattern in green, including "raspberries." **No mark.** Kingussie, Highland folk Museum, Highland Council. £80, $160.

592. Bowl. c. 7" (17.8 cm). Two green lines enclose a row of "strawberries" in the form of a small sponge in red, yellow and green. **No mark.** Collection: Hunterian Museum, University of Glasgow. £95, $190.

Decorative Flowers

The following group shows pieces in which a great part of the decoration shows flowers, either painted or sponge printed. The group is notable as being very large. This probably indicated the imaginative scope of the English potters who certainly made most of the pieces in the group but could equally well reflect the taste of the American public of the period for which most of these pieces were intended. Some slight evidence for this statement comes from the fact that most of these are taken from the Durrie photographs.

At the same time, it is unfortunate that Durrie was unable to indicate the place of original find for many of the pieces since quite a number of them look like export pieces for Asia.

593. Plate. 8.5" (21.6 cm). The daisy motifs are green with purple centers. A loosely textured sponge was used. The daisy motif is common on plates with a painted center and many color variants are known. **No mark.** £80, $160.

594. Plate. 7.5" (19.1 cm). Three pale blue lines. Between the two outer ones are red flowers with green leaves; between the two inner there is red foliage. **No mark.** £90, $180.

595. Plate. 6.5" (16.5 cm). Very similar to pieces shown by Finlayson and Scottish in origin. **No mark.** £70, $140.

596. Plate. 8.5" (21.6 cm). Two bands of red flowers and green leaves with red lines. **No mark.** £40, $80.

597. Plate. 8.625" (21.0 cm). Flow blue sponged daisies and hearts with a central daisy. **No mark.** £50, $100.

598. Plate. 8.75" (22 cm). Four red lines and blue/green and red flowers. **No mark.** £40, $80.

599. Plate. 4.125" (10.5 cm). Red flowers and paired blue diamond shapes alternate with paired green leaves. Part of a child's tea set. A common variant of **PERSIAN ROSE**. **No mark.** £40, $80.

600. Plate. 4.75" (12.1 cm). A molded holly border with six red sponged flowers. The large central flower is framed by green foliage. **No mark.** £35, $70.

601. Saucer. Outer red and inner green motifs. **No mark.** £50, $100.

602. Plate. 5.25" (13.1 cm). A black rim with blue flowers and foliage and red dots. Part of a child's large tea set or more likely a cabaret. **No mark.** £40, $80.

603. Plate. 7.325" (18.6 cm). The plate is molded into ten panels, each with a flower made of green dots round a red one. The same motif is used in the central well but this has outer green and inner red dots round a green central dot. Petra Williams calls this **"Dot Flower"** in *Flow Blue China II*. It is also known on "an enormous covered sugar bowl." £60, $120.

604. Saucer. A blue line surrounds red flowers and green leaves. It was bought in Rhode Island and a matching cup was found in Ohio which gives some idea of the travels of this ware, either in older or more modern times. **No mark.** £50, $100.

605. Saucer. On each spray is a large red flower, two smaller blue flowers and a pair of green leaves. **No mark.** £50, $100.

606. Plate. 10" (25.4 cm). All in brown. **No mark.** £40, $80.

607. Cup and saucer. Red lines with green, sponge printed "stars" and blue rings. **No mark.** £60, $120.

608. Cup and saucer. Blue lines. A complex sponge in red, green and brown. The wielder of the sponge had some skill. **No mark.** £65, $130.

609. Cup and saucer. Red lines with green foliage and red flowers. **No mark.** £60, $120.

610. Cup and saucer. Blue lines and brown sponge printed flowers with green leaves. **No mark.** £40, $80.

611. Cup and saucer. Red rim line, then black lines on either side of a yellow band. Sponge printed blue daisies. Other pieces are known with the same pattern but marked **MADE IN ENGLAND,** which would place them after 1891. £50, $100.

612. Child's cup and saucer. The outer band is red and the inner green. **No mark.** £60, $120.

613. Cup and saucer. Red lines flank a blue band with sponge printed deep blue flowers. **No mark.** £45, $90.

614. Cup and saucer. Both have red flowers and green leaves but they do not match. **No mark.** £25, $50.

615. Cup and saucer. Green lines and blue sponged flowers with green leaves. **No mark.** £30, $60.

616. Child's cup and saucer. Red and blue sponged flowers with green leaves. **No mark.** £30, $60.

617. Cup. A green rim line with red motifs. **No mark.** £40, $80.

618. Cup. Five colors. The rim line and round, spoked flowers are red, the paired "lilies" with two leaves are blue, the triangles are yellow and the second lily-like flower with leaves is green. The central line is black. **No mark.** £70, $140.

619. Cup. A green rim line with two sets of five red flowers and three green leaves. **No mark.** £70, $140.

620. Bowl. 4.75" (12.1 cm). The sponged flowers are blue and seem to show Oriental influence. **No mark.** £90, $180.

621. Bowl. 5.25" (13.3 cm). The top band has red motifs, the lower band blue and green. It came from Canada. **No mark.** £80, $160.

622. Bowl. 6.25" (15.9 cm). **No mark.** £75, $150.

623. Sugar basin. 5 x 5" (12.7 cm). Blue bows and red daisies in alternating columns. A porous sponge has been used. **No mark.** £50, $100.

624. Bowl. 5.25" (13.3 cm). Three red bands and blue sponge printed motifs. This has been copied in modern times. **No mark.** £60, $120.

625. Bowl. 6.25" (15.9 cm). Black lines enclose a top row of red and a bottom row of blue motifs. **No mark.** £90, $180.

626. Child's cup and saucer. A blue rim line, red flowers, and green leaves, the two latter with a connecting black line. **No mark.** £80, $160.

627. Mug. 3.25" (8.3 cm). A red line and green sponge prints. **No mark.** £120, $240.

628. Bowl. Heart-shaped motifs in blue form bands at rim and base, while between are three-color floral motifs. The flower resembles a species of thistle. **No mark.** £60, $120.

629. Mug. 3.5" (8.3 cm). The rim motif is red, the flowers are red with yellow centers, and the foliage is green with yellow tips. Coupled sponges were used with more than one color. **No mark.** £110, $220.

630. Salt box. 4.25" (11.4 cm). It would store salt hanging from a nail by the fire to prevent damp and would have a wooden lid. Sponge printed in blue. **No mark.** £100, $200.

631. Mug. 2.75" (6.9 cm). Red flowers and green foliage. **No mark.** £80, $160.

632. Tureen. 11 x 8 x 6.5" (27.9 x 20.3 x 16.5 cm). The pattern was called **Bulls-eye** Variant 3 or **Christmas Bullseye** because of the flow blue holly leaves. It also has red bells, blue lines, red holly berries and green florets. **No mark.** £40, $80.

633. Ewer. 12" (30.5 cm). Red line with red flower and green foliage. **No mark.** £90, $180.

634. Cup with no handle. Green lines and a complex red sponged motif. **No mark.** £50, $100.

635. Cup and saucer. A red line with arched brown leaf sponge and purple flowers. **No mark.** £130, $260.

636. Bowl. 6.25" (15.9 cm). An inner and three outer black lines. Red leaves and flowers in the top row, blue leaves in the bottom row. The base has an impressed crown. £80, $160.

637. Bowl. 5.625" (14.3 cm). Large red flowers, green leaves with brown stems, all between red lines. Stylistically, this looks late and would date from after 1900. **No mark.** £50, $100.

638. Sugar basin and cream jug. **"Snowflakes"** in red. **No mark.** £45, $90.

639. Bowl. 6" (15.2 cm). Two red lines enclose a blue floral border. Below this large red and small blue flowers with green leaves are joined by a thin black line. **No mark.** £60, $120.

640. Child's cup and saucer. Black lines with red flowers and green leaves. **No mark.** £20, $40.

641. Cup. 4.25" (10.8 cm). Red lines and red flowers with green leaves. **No mark.** £50, $100.

642. Child's cup and saucer. Blue lines, a yellow band with black top and blue bottom rows of motifs. **No mark.** £70, $140.

643. Saucer. Brown dot flowers with green centers. **No mark.** £70, $140.

644. Cup. A top row of overlapping alternate red and green motifs. The bottom row is of blue diamonds. **No mark.** £85, $170.

645. Bowl. 12 x 3". Faience. Blue sponged flowers, stencils and brushstroke. **No mark.** £35, $70.

646. Cup and saucer. Red lines with alternating red and blue "stars." The stars on the cup are six-pointed while those on the saucer are eight-pointed and have a central dot; this may be a marriage. **No mark.** £65, $130.

647. Bowl with beaded rim. 10.75" (27.3 cm). Green lines enclose a deep blue band. Green sponge printing with red flowers. Probably Scottish. **No mark.** £80, $160.

648. Child's saucer. 4.5" (15.2 cm). Blue lines. The outer circle is red, the inner has alternating yellow flowers and green leaves. **No mark.** £60, $120.

649. Cup and saucer. Green lines enclose red flowers and leaves. **No mark.** £120, $240.

650. Saucer. 6″ (15.2 cm). The outer ring is a red sponge print on a red line. The inner ring has green crosses. **No mark.** £110, $220.

651. Carpet bowls. These were used in an indoor game popular, and perhaps originating, in Scotland. Usually one set of bowls was sponge printed and the other painted with crossing lines. There was a smaller white jack. They were of solid clay and were made universally in Scotland and Northern England. There is no way to ascribe them meaningfully to a particular pottery since they are never marked; but collectors should beware since there are many modern imitations being passed off as antiques. Diameters vary from 2.5″ to 3.5″ (6.3 to 8.9 cm), but the standard size is 3.25″ (8.3 cm). The chapter in Baumann contains several errors of fact but is still useful. £35, $70.

652. Pitcher. All decoration in brown. By its shape this should be Scottish and date from c. 1890. **No mark.** £30, $60.

653. Bowl with beaded rim, one of a pair. The lines and the outer band are in red, then there is a band of blue 'wheels' and a central red flower with green leaves. **No mark.** £35, $70.

654. Saucer. Blue lines, red flowers, green leaves. **No mark.** £200, $400.

655. Cup. Dark green lines inside and outside the rim. Two groups of red flower and green leaves with a single green leaf between. **No mark.** £45, $90.

656. Saucer. Red line, green leaves, large red and small blue flowers. **No mark.** £50, $100.

657. Child's tea set. All decoration in brown. Basket-like forms, each containing three tulips hanging inverted from a line. **No mark.** £90, $180.

658. Saucer. A red line with sponged blue flowers and green leaves joined by a thin black line. **No mark.** £70, $140.

659. Bowl. 6.5" (16.5 cm). A green border of horizontal flowers and a lower band of red flowers with green leaves. **No mark.** £45, $90.

660. Cup, saucer and tea plate. Inner and outer bands are in blue; the middle band has pink/purple thistles alternating with brown "wheels." **No mark.** £50, $100.

661. Mug. 4" (10.2 cm). Red with blue flowers. **No mark.** £60, $120.

662. Bowl. 6.125" (15.7 cm). Brown lines with sponged red flowers and green leaves between. Bought in Dublin which could well indicate a Scottish origin, but the general style does not look Scottish. **No mark.** £60, $120.

663. Cup and saucer. Green lines and leaves with red flowers. **No mark.** £65, $130.

664. Bowl. 5.875" (14.9 cm). An upper band of green leaves and flowers. A lower band in blue. Bought in Ireland. **No mark.** £40, $80.

665. Mug. 2.875" (7.2 cm). Red lines and flower with green leaves. **No mark.** £70, $140.

666. Mug. 3.125″ (7.9 cm). Blue flowers with red stems. **No mark.** £55, $110.

667. Cup. Red flowers and blue dots on a thin green line. **No mark.** £65, $130.

668. Bowl. 6.25″ (15.9 cm). Black line. An upper band in red motifs and a lower in blue/green. **No mark.** £85, $170.

669. Cup and saucer. An upper band of green flowers and leaves and a lower band of red crosses. **No mark.** £30, $60.

670. Cup and saucer. Red lines and flowers with leaves in two shades of green. **No mark**. £60, $120.

671. Plate. 11.125" (28.3 cm). An outer blue line. Pink flowers and green leaves are joined by black lines. **It has an impressed mark probably for J.S. Moore & Co. See Mark no. 671A.** £100, $200.

671A

672. Child's cup. Alternate red and green motifs. **No mark.** £60, $120.

673. Bowl. 8" (20.3 cm). The top band is in pale blue. Below this are five complex prints of red flowers and green foliage. **No mark.** £90, $180.

674. Plate. 10″ (25.4 cm). The border is purple with every other flower overstamped in red. A brown central basket has blue and red flowers and green and brown foliage in a complex sponge. The six sprays have red flowers and red and green foliage. A very elaborate, skilful piece which would be relatively expensive. **No mark.** £1100, $2200.

675. Bowl. 7.75″ (19.7 cm). A blue border band. Four red flowers with green foliage. **No mark.** £90, $180.

676. Bowl. 9.875″ (25.1 cm). Red lines and flowers with other motifs in blue. **No mark.** £80, $160.

677. Bowl of heavy earthenware. 11″ (27.9 cm). **No mark.** £60, $120.

678. Bowl. 8″ (20.3 cm). On the outside is a band of blue flowers and leaves. Inside, the central flower is made up of seven blue units. The smaller flowers are red and the foliage green. **No mark.** £150, $300.

679. Mug. 4″ (10.2 cm) All decoration in brown sponge printing. **No mark.** £90, $180.

680. Bowl. 5.5″ (14 cm). A red line at the rim. On either side is a group of red flowers and green foliage. There is one red flower in the bottom of the bowl. **No mark.** £70, $140.

681. Ewer and basin. Ewer 12.5″ (31.8 cm), basin 13″ (33 cm). Red lines and flowers. Green leaves. **No mark.** £65, $130.

682. Plate. 8.75" (22 cm). Green lines with a purple outer band and a brown inner one. **No mark.** £75, $150.

683. Cup and saucer. Blue lines and red flowers with green foliage, all joined by a black line. **No mark.** £65, $130.

684. Bowl. 6.375" (16.2 cm). A top band in blue and four units of blue flowers with green foliage. **No mark.** £55, $110.

685. Bowl. 7" (17.8 cm). Three cable bands in brown — one midway down the outside. The other sponge motifs are in blue. Most decoration is in the interior. **No mark.** £70, $140.

686. Alphabet plate. 6.75″ (17.1 cm). The central flower is brown and the radiating foliage green. **No mark.** £100, $200.

687. Bowl. 6.625″ (16.8 cm). A rim band and flowers in red. Green leaves. **No mark.** £100, $200.

688. Soup plate. 10.75″ (27.3 cm). All in blue. **No mark.** £40, $80.

689 and 690. Frog mug. 4.25″ (10.8 cm). Exterior: an upper band in blue and a lower in red. **No mark.** £70, $140.

691. Saucer. 5.75" (14.6 cm). Blue lines and green sponged motifs. Very deep. **No mark.** £65, $130.

692. Mug. 4" (10.2 cm). A multicolored sponge print with the lower part pink and the upper brown. **No mark.** £40, $80.

693. Bowl. 7" (17.8 cm). Purple lines enclose red flowers, blue florets and green leaves. **No mark.** £50, $100.

694. Mug. 4" (10.2 cm). All decoration is in brown with three flowers. **No mark.** £50, $100.

695. Bowl. 6.125" (15.7 cm). A red line, blue flowers and larger red motifs. **No mark.** £40, $80.

696. Cup and saucer. Green rim lines. Purple flowers and green leaves are connected by a black line. **No mark.** £45, $90.

697. Bowl. 6" (15.2 cm). Green lines and painted leaves. The sponged flowers are blue. **No mark.** £45, $90.

698. Plate. 8.875" (22.4 cm). Sponge printed triangles in red and florets in blue with painted green leaves. **No mark.** £60, $120.

699. Plate. 6.875" (17.5 cm). **PERSIAN ROSE** painted in red and green with blue sponge printed florets. **No mark.** £50, $100.

700. Saucer. A cross between **VIRGINIA** and **PERSIAN ROSE**. Red and green painting, sponge printing in pale blue. **No mark.** £80, $160.

701. Plate. The only sponge printed elements are the "flowers." **No mark.** £120, $240.

702. Rice dish. 9.25" (23.5 cm). The outer band has red and blue flowers, green foliage and sponge printed purple florets. The center has the same without the florets. **No mark.** £40, $80.

703. Plate. 9.875" (25.1 cm). Blue lines, red bows and a painted red rose with green foliage and blue flowers. **No mark.** £40, $80.

704. Plate. 10" (25.4 cm). Red lines enclose a blue sponged border. The **THREE PLUM** pattern. Plums and light green foliage are painted while dark green leaves and blue florets are sponged. **No mark.** £80, $160.

705. Plate. 6.375" (16.2 cm). Blue lines enclose red and green florets. The painted central motif is of red flowers and green leaves. **No mark.** £70, $140.

706. Plate. 7" (17.8 cm). Painted red lines and green leaves, sponged blue "snowflakes" and red florets. It is known with reversed sponge colors. **No mark.** £75, $150.

Top left: 707. Plate. 9.5" (24.1 cm). Blue lines enclose a sponged red border. The middle has green foliage, blue flowers and red flares, the very center being red and blue. A derivative of **GARDEN**. **No mark.** £110, $220.

Top right: 708. Plate. 7" (17.8 cm). Green lines with a band of red leaves and blue flowers. **No mark.** £100, $200.

Center left: 709. Bowl. 10.125" (25.7 cm). The sponged motif inside the molded, beaded border is blue as is the middle flower. The other flowers are red and the foliage green and yellow. **No mark.** £100, $200.

Center right: 710. Soup plate. 10" (25.4 cm). Black lines enclose the red sponging on the flange. The center is hand-painted in blue, green and pink. This and the following two plates are typical of the wares exported to Asia, as is 705. It would be interesting to know where they were first found. **No mark.** £130, $260.

Bottom right: 711. Plate. 9.375" (23.7 cm). Red lines and swags; green leaves in the center and brown sponge printed flowers. **No mark.** £140, $280.

712. Soup plate. 8.5" (21.6 cm). Red lines and swags, purple pendant flowers and blue florets with green foliage. Purple sponge printing. **No mark.** £55, $110.

713. Plate. 10" (25.4 cm). Robacker's **Bullseye** pattern. Red sponged flowers, etc. on the border and red florets round the center. The other sponged florets are green. All the other elements, sponged and painted, are flow blue. **No mark.** £45, $90.

714. Plate. 10" (25.4 cm). Red and green sponge printing on the rim, elsewhere there are red flowers and green florets. Flow blue lines and painted leaves. **No mark.** £50, $100.

715. Cup and saucer. Red lines, blue sponged border and red and blue painted buds with green leaves, all loosely textured. **No mark.** £55, $110.

716. Cup and saucer. Red lines and sponged flowers, green painted leaves. **No mark.** £50, $100.

717. Cup and saucer. A variant of **PERSIAN ROSE** in the usual colors. **No mark.** £45, $90.

718. Cup and saucer. Red lines and painted masses; blue sponge printed flowers with green painted leaves and detached brown leaves. **No mark.** £40, $80.

719. Cup and saucer. Groups of sponged flowers are alternately red and blue; the painted leaves are green **No mark.** £25, $50.

720. Cup and saucer. A really distant derivative of **PERSIAN ROSE**. Painted red flowers and leaves in two shades of green. Small blue sponged florets. **No mark.** £40, $80.

721. Cup and saucer. They are similar but not matching. The cup has red florets; the saucer red and blue florets. **No mark.** £45, $90.

722. Cup. Red sponge printed florets and painted green leaves. **No mark.** £45, $90.

723. Cup and saucer. Red and blue sponge printed florets. **No mark.** £70, $140.

724. Cup and saucer. The sponged groups are alternately red and blue with green painted leaves. **No mark.** £95, $190.

725. Bowl. 6.375" (16.2 cm). Red flowers, green foliage and sponged blue florets. **No mark.** £80, $160.

726. Breakfast cup and saucer. Cup is 6" (15.2 cm) in diameter. Robacker's **Bullseye** variant 4. The flow blue leaves are painted. Blue lines. The sponged bands are alternately red and green, the florets green, the flowers red. **No mark.** £100, $200.

727. Molded bowl. 11" (27.9 cm). All in flow blue and all sponged except for the lines and the pendant "leaves." A derivative of **GARDEN**. **No mark.** £150, $300.

728. Plate. 8.75" (22 cm). A painted center with a purple and yellow flower and green foliage. Red lines and green sponge printed motifs. **No mark.** £140, $280.

729. Soup plate? 8.25" (20.9 cm). Lines in red, green and yellow. The border and central florets are sponge printed in blue and there are painted red flowers with green centers and foliage. **No mark.** £90, $180.

730. Plate. 8.875" (22.4 cm). Red lines and a green sponge printed border. The central flower is purple with red buds, blue blossoms and green foliage. Similar plates are impressed **HARVEY**. **No mark** on this. £100, $200.

731. Plate. 8.5" (21.6 cm). Red flower and lines, green foliage, purple sponge printed bows. **No mark.** £120, $240.

732. Plate. 8.5″ (21.6 cm). Like 728 but the sponged border is blue. **No mark.** £100, $200.

733. Plate. 8.5″ (21.6 cm). Blue lines, red sponged bows, two sponged flowers and a painted flower and bud. The painted foliage is green. This is sometimes referred to (in the U.S.A. only) as **"Columbine and Thistle." No mark.** £160, $320.

734. Ewer. 13″ (33 cm). Yellow lines. The sponged band is red. The main band (the large foliage clumps) are red and the rest green. The sponge printed florets are blue. **No mark.** £30, $60.

735. Plate. 9.5″ (24.1 cm). Red lines, green sponged bows, painting in red and green. **No mark.** £40, $80.

736. Sugar basin. 7" x 7.75" (17.8 x 19.7 cm). Blue lines, purple bows and painting in red and green. **No mark.** £130, $260.

737. Child's (or coffee) saucer. 4.375" (11.1 cm). Black lines and painted leaves. The round flowers are blue, the others red. **No mark.** £75, $150.

738. Bowl. 4" (10.2 cm). Red lines and painted buds, green foliage and sponged blue flowers. **No mark.** £35, $70.

739. Rice dish. 10.25" (26 cm). The rim line is purple and the others are blue. The outer sponged band is red, painted foliage is green with blue and yellow sponged and red, purple and blue painted flowers. This dish was certainly meant for the Asian market; it would be interesting to know if it ever reached its destination. **No mark.** £35, $70.

740. Cup and saucer. Blue lines, bows in red, and purple and yellow flower. Durrie called this the **Pansy Pattern** but seems to have meant just the central element. **No mark.** £50, $100.

741. Bowl. 4.125" (10.5 cm). Green lines, painted red and green foliage and blue and yellow sponge printed flowers. **No mark.** £75, $150.

742. Saucer. Red rim line, painted green foliage and red flowers. Sponged blue flowers. An odd version of **PERSIAN ROSE**. **No mark.** £30, $60.

743. Cup and saucer. Red and green painting, blue sponge printing. Another crude version of **PERSIAN ROSE**. **No mark.** £75, $150.

744. Plate. 8.75" (22 cm). Red lines, blue sponge printed border. A pink painted flower with green leaves. **No mark.** £135, $270.

745. Saucer. Red sponged florets and green painted foliage. **No mark.** £30, $60.

746. Bowl. 8.25" (20.3 cm). Blue lines enclosed crimson and green triangles. Centrally there are crimson flowers, blue florets and green leaves. From Indonesia. **Mark: Shield with F & O.** £45, $90.

747. Plate. 10.5" (26.7 cm). Five swags of blue sponged florets, each enclose a red flower hanging from the rim line. At the joins of the swags are green twigs partly sponge printed and partly painted. **No mark.** £70, $140.

748. Saucer. Green painted foliage. Triple sponged florets in red and painted in blue. **No mark.** £140, $280.

749. Bowl. 6.75" (17.1 cm). A broad band of brown and black. Red sponged flowers with blue centers, blue dots and green foliage. There is a large red flower in the interior. **No mark.** £110, $220.

750. Breakfast cup. 5.75" (14.6 cm). The bands are blue with flecks of black. Red sponged florets alternate with blue sponged motifs. **No mark.** £30, $60.

751. Plate. 9.5" (24.1 cm). Blue lines enclose a purple sponged border. Swags are blue with enclosed yellow spaces and sponged black motifs. Red, green, blue and yellow are all used in the central painted area. Bought in England. **No mark.** £100, $200.

752. Rice dish. 11.5" (29.2 cm). All in red and sponge printed except for the central foliage. **No mark.** £130, $260.

753. Cup. Green lines enclose red sponged dots and painted green leaves. **No mark.** £95, $190.

754. Covered mug. 6.25" (15.3 cm). A red sponged band and blue sponged flowers. Lines and stems are painted in blue, foliage in green and flares in red and blue. **No mark.** £185, $370.

755. Dish. 12.5" (31.8 cm). Green lines enclose a red sponged border. The crossed bands are red with sponged yellow florets on them. In each quarter there are three blue sponged florets, black lines and painted green foliage. The central circle is red. **No mark.** £70, $140.

756. Soup plate. 10.5" (26.7 cm). **VIRGINIA** with a decorated center. Purple sponged florets. Painted flowers in red and blue with green foliage. **No mark.** £150, $300.

757. Platter or ashet. 13.5 x 10.5" (34.3 x 26.7 cm). Red lines enclose blue daisies with no centers. **No mark.** £100, $200.

758. Cup and saucer. Red lines enclose green sponged daisies. The center is purple and blue with green foliage. **No mark.** £120, $240.

759. Charger. 14" (35.6 cm). **VIRGINIA** with a decorated center. Purple sponged florets. **No mark.** £40, $80.

760. Serving dish. 12.5 x 2.25" (31.89 x 5.7 cm). The border is sponge printed in red and the central bouquet has red roses and buds, blue flowers and green foliage. **No mark.** £55, $110.

761. Rice dish. 10.125" (25.7 cm). Black lines enclose red sponged motifs. Black knots are in yellow areas bounded by swags. A painted center. The knots are examples of the Staffordshire Knot which could give a clue as to origin. **No mark.** £65, $130.

762. Cup and saucer. Red lines and painted flowers, green foliage, sponged blue florets. **No mark.** £120, $240.

763. Tea plate. Red painted flowers with green foliage and blue sponged flowers. **No mark.** £60, $120.

Top left: 764. Bowl. 8.5" (21.6 cm). Broad blue lines with black sponged motifs. A central red flower. **No mark.** £150, $300.

Top right: 765. Rice dish. 9.375" (23.7 cm). Red swags and lines, blue sponged border, blue flares, triple sponged blue florets and green painted foliage. **No mark.** £45, $90.

Center left: 766. Mug. 4.375" (11.1 cm). Bands of black, yellow, blue and red at the top. Red and blue sponge printed flowers and green leaves along a black line in the middle. **No mark.** £85, $170.

Center right: 767. Flask. 8" (20.3 cm). Central sponge printed flowers in red and outer flowers in purple. All the foliage is green. **No mark.** £200, $400.

Bottom right: 768. Child's cup and saucer. Red line and sponged flowers with green painted foliage. **No mark.** £40, $80.

Top left: 769. Plate. 9.75" (24.7 cm). Four red sponge printed flowers with green foliage and blue sponge printing. **No mark.** £50, $100.

Top right: 770. Rice dish. 16.75" (42.5 cm). The **PLUM PATTERN**. Red plums. Red lines enclose a blue sponged border. **No mark.** This is a truly magnificent size and must have been an export dish. It would have been good to have found where it came from. £100, $200.

Center left: 771. Bowl. 3.75" (9.5 cm). Gray sponged flowers, blue foliage and green painted leaves. **No mark.** £95, $190.

Center right: 772. Cup and saucer. Crimson flowers, flares and lines, and blue and green painting. **No mark.** £70, $140.

Bottom right: 773. Three piece butter dish. 5.5" high (14 cm). **VIRGINIA** with blue sponge printed flowers. The large flowers have green sepals. **No mark.** Green sepals sometimes appear on Baker's **VIRGINIA**. £80, $160.

Top left: 774. Wash bowl. 14 x 4.75" (35.6 x 12.1 cm). **VIRGINIA** with green sepals. **No mark.** £90, $180.

Top right: 775. Bowl. 5.625" (14.3 cm). Blue lines enclose blue dabbing overlaid with sponge printed green leaves and pink and blue flowers. **No mark.** £90, $180.

Center left: 776. Cup and saucer. Red sponge printed flowers and green leaves overlie a rather primitive sponge printed yellow dabbed ground. **No mark.** £60, $120.

Center right: 777. Sauce boat & underdish. Crimson, blue, green, black and yellow all present. **No mark** but almost certainly **Auld Heather Ware.** £70, $140.

Bottom right: 778. Rice dish. 11.875" (30.1 cm). Red dabbing with sponge printed blue and green motifs. Almost a piece of "careful dabbing." **No mark.** £45, $90.

Top left: 779. Bowl. 6.875″ (17.5 cm). Brown lines flank a dabbed band overlaid with blue and green sponge printed floral motifs. **No mark.** £40, $80.

Top right: 780. Bowl. 5.5″ (14 cm). An internal brown line. Externally bands of brown dabbing with sponge printed floral motifs in red, purple and blue. **No mark.** £80, $160.

Center left: 781. Plate. 8.5″ (21.6 cm). Red dabbing round the rim and sponge printed "snowflakes." **No mark.** £60, $120.

Center right: 782. Plate. 8.875″ (22.4 cm). Green dabbing at the rim and green sponge printing. **No mark.** £75, $150.

Bottom right: 783. Plate. 8.625″ (21.9 cm). A band of diamonds in blue and double ovals in green. The inner band is red. There is an illegible impressed mark. £80, $160.

784. Tea bowl and saucer. An upper sponge printed band in green and a lower in red. An illegible mark. £90, $180.

785. Teapot stand. 6.875" (17.5 cm). Pink lines. Floral units in pink and green, others in blue. There is an illegible mark. This piece may well be stencilled rather than sponge printed. £110, $220.

786. Bowl. c. 7" (17.8 cm). Two green lines enclose a complex sponge print of thistles shown on a slight diagonal. **No mark** but perhaps Scottish. £90, $180.

787. Soup plate. c. 8" (20.3 cm). Three blue lines. The first two enclose a leaflike motif in red. Between two and three is a complex, floral motif in red and light green. This plate has a stamped black mark with a coat of arms and a pottery description which is indecipherable apart from the word **GLASGOW**. Subsequently another piece was found with the same mark in transfer print. **This proved to be the mark for Cowie Bros., a Glasgow firm of exporter/importers and not a pottery mark.** Collection: Hunterian Museum, University of Glasgow. £70, $140.

788. Rice dish. c. 8" (20.3 cm). Crimson lines enclose seven black printed motifs alternating with seven blue rectangles with crimson edging. Centrally there is a painted flower with three crimson petals. **No mark.** Collection: Hunterian Museum, University of Glasgow. £55, $110.

790. Textured bowl. c. 6.5″ (16.5 cm). A crimson line beneath which is a band of blue flowers then a complex, floral sponge in crimson and green. **No mark.** Collection: Hunterian Museum, University of Glasgow. £75, $150.

789. Soup plate. c. 8″ (20.3 cm). Printed with two sponges: one in blue showing a flower and a cross; the other in violet showing a sort of Greek key. **No mark.** Collection: Hunterian Museum, University of Glasgow. £70, $140.

791. Two mugs. c. 4″ (10.2 cm). All over designs in blue and crimson. The prints are sometimes only partially on the body, showing the lack of care in making the ware. **No mark.** Collection: Hunterian Museum, University of Glasgow. £65, $130.

792. Bowl. An abstract print in blue used at the rim; below this is a band of floral motifs printed in crimson. The blue is in a loosely textured sponge, the crimson is much firmer. **No mark.** £75, $150.

793. Bowl. Around the middle of the bowl is a wavy line in blue. Below this is a band of complex motifs in green and crimson. The same motif is used above the band but presented alternately vertically and horizontally. **No mark.** £100, $200.

Top left: 794. Bowl. Three motifs are used, all rather crudely cut. Blue at and off the rim, crimson flowers and green foliage. **No mark.** Collection: Kingussie, the Highland Folk Museum, Highland Council, Scotland. £85, $170.

Top right: 795. Mug. A rim band of blue flowers. Below this is an abstract motif in two colors, crimson and olive. Fochabers Museum, Fochabers, Scotland. **No mark.** £65, $130.

Center left: 796. Soup plate. A band of black including fleur-de-lis, then a tiny crimson motif, then the same with green leaves surrounds a black line and a crimson **"Glasgow Rose." No mark.** £40, $80.

Center right: 797. Rice dish. A blue approximation to the **"Glasgow Rose"** has links of a double green chain and brown/red leaves. This pattern is found quite often in Scotland but is never marked. Collection: Hunterian Museum, University of Glasgow. £40, $80.

Bottom left: 798. Bowl. c. 5" (12.7 cm). Two olive lines enclose a "Ball flower" in purple with orange/brown leaves and similar doubled flowers. This motif is found on a fair number of different pieces in many different color combinations. **No mark.** Collection: Hunterian Museum, University of Glasgow. £50, $100.

Bottom right: 799. Bowl. c. 4" (10.2 cm). Decorated entirely in gray, a color which became very popular in the later 1870s. Round the rim is a carelessly applied band of trefoils and below this a flower and leaf alternates with a completely undecipherable sponge. This is typical of the sort of wares that were sent to out of the way parts of Scotland in the late 19th century. **No mark.** £70, $140.

800. Two mugs. c. 5" (12.7 cm). One decorated in faint blue with a rim band and scattered floral motifs on the body; the other with a shaded brown rim and green swags. These are typical of the bottom of the market English wares (cf. previous entry-799). **No marks.** £125, $250 & £95, $190.

801. Detail of mug. c. 5.5" (14 cm). Allover decoration in brown. It is difficult to determine how many sponges were used here but it is probably only one which has four elements and a mistake which seems to have been corrected at one point. **No mark.** £95, $190.

802. Ashet or platter. c. 10" (25.4 cm). A dark purple floral motif decorates the rim and the edge of the well. **No mark.** Collection: Hunterian Museum, University of Glasgow. £40, $80.

803. Pitcher. c. 8" (20.3 cm). A blue "fringed wheel" forms bands at the rim and base and each side has a complex sponge with a crimson flower and green leaves. **No mark.** Collection: Ulster Folk and Transport Museum, NMGNI. £50, $100.

804. Pitcher. c. 8" (20.3 cm). Red/brown lines at rim, belly and base. Below the first is a band of leaflike motifs; below the second a band of floral motifs, both in light blue. Collection: Hunterian Museum, University of Glasgow. £60, $120.

805. Two mugs. c. 3.5″ and 4.5″ (8.9 and 11.4 cm). Similarly and simply decorated with two rows of crimson and green flowers. **No mark.** Collection: Ulster Folk and Transport Museum, NMGNI. £50, $100.

807. Two-handled mug. c. 4.5″ (11.4 cm). A rim band of fairly crude floral motifs in brown. **No mark.** Collection: Hunterian Museum, University of Glasgow. £70, $140.

809. Mug. Pink flowers with a dense green surround alternate with blue floral posies in pairs. Flowers of this kind have been found on a dump of rather late material from Britannia Pottery, Glasgow. This dump also contained sherds of the wares with Quebec views made for M.C. Thomas (Finlayson). **No mark.** Collection: Ulster Folk and Transport Museum, NMGNI. £45, $90.

806. Bowl. c. 5″ (12.7 cm). A band of brown sponge printing at the rim, vaguely botanical. Below are a few complex sponges in blue, gray and pink. **No mark.** Collection: Kingussie, the Highland Folk Museum, Highland Council. £85, $170.

808. Mug. c. 3.5″ (8.9 cm). A red rim stripe is the only decoration save for a complex sponge on each side in pink, brown and blue, showing two flowers on a twig. **No mark.** Collection: Hunterian Museum, University of Glasgow. £85, $170.

810. Bowl. Blue flowers joined by double green chain, each flower having three orange leaflets. **No mark.** Collection: Hunterian Museum, University of Glasgow. (cf. 780). £60, $120.

811. Bowl. c. 8″ (20.3 cm). Slight carination. At rim and carination there are bands of blue double chain. Between are red and green flowers with green leaves in a complex sponge. **No mark** but certainly Scottish. Collection: Hunterian Museum, University of Glasgow. £65, $130.

812. Small bowl. c. 3″ (7.6 cm). Two double lines in blue/gray enclose alternating flowers in blue and crosses in green/gray. Very unusual coloring. **No mark.** Collection: Hunterian Museum, University of Glasgow. £60, $120.

813. Two bowls. Both bowls were decorated in gray, which dates them most probably after 1875. Both have a rim band in one design and a different design under this. Ulster Folk and Transport Museum, NMGNI. £80, $160.

814. Bowl. Two bands of sponges. First blue flowers, then red "leaves." **No mark.** £45, $90.

815. Bowl. A crimson line at rim from which hang blue trefoils. Lower are crimson and green flowers. **No mark.** Collection: Fochabers Museum, Fochabers, Scotland. £45, $90.

816. Bowl. Flow blue throughout. Thick lines enclose panels with flowers, fans, etc. **No mark.** £50, $100.

817. Bowl. A blue rim line and blue flowers in two staggered rows. **No mark.** £75, $150.

818. Bowl. The rim has brown double chain with intervening rings. Body has crimson and green flowers. **No mark.** Collection: Kingussie, the Highland Folk Museum, Highland Council. £50, $100.

819. Bowl, molded with a leaf pattern. Decoration in blue consists of flower sponges between the moldings and a rim band with another floral sponge. **No mark.** Collection: Kingussie, the Highland Folk Museum, Highland Council. £45, $90.

820. Bowl. Band of brown leaves in sponge at rim and near base. Between large blue flowers alternate with dark green leaves. **No mark.** £40, $80.

821. Bowl. A band of red flowers, very carelessly applied, at the rim. Below that, a complex sponge in gray and red of a not very decipherable object which appears to be both animal and vegetable. **No mark.** Collection: Fochabers Museum, Fochabers, Scotland. £40, $80.

822. Bowl with spout. A most unusual shape. The woven pattern on the molded bowl is completely ignored by the rather crude floral motifs in dark green and brown. **No mark.** £80, $160.

The remaining pieces are completely miscellaneous, no attempt has been made to dragoon them into groups of any kind.

Left to right, top to bottom:
823. Plate. 8.75" (22 cm). This pattern is known in purple, in blue and in a combination of the two. It has been given several names in the past. SNOWFLAKE seems the most appropriate. Two pieces are known marked SB but remain unidentified. **No mark.** £90, $180.

824. Tea plate. 6.625" (16.8 cm). Sponge printed in blue. **No mark.** £70, $140.

825. Plate. 8.375" (21 cm). A border of green daisies without centers. The bow pattern is red, the lining blue. **No mark.** £50, $100.

826. Plate. 8.75" (22 cm). A black Greek key border and black leaves. The center is red with blue and green lining. **No mark.** £45, $90.

827. Plate. 6.3" (16 cm). Very carefully printed so that the motifs fit perfectly. The three bands from the rim are blue/green, light green and yellow. **No mark.** £55, $110.

828. Plate. 8.875" (22.4 cm). Black line. The red motifs alternate with green and yellow. **No mark.** £50, $100.

Top left: 829. Plate. 9" (22.9 cm). Green motifs hang from a red line. Sherds of this type were found in Glasgow in a mixed dump of wasters from Britannia and Glasgow Potteries. **No mark.** £60, $120.

Top right: 830. Plate. 8.75" (22 cm). A ring of black Greek key. The middle band is green and the inner red. **No mark.** £55, $110.

Center left: 831. Plate. 8.625" (21.8 cm). Green lines and a band of green, blue and yellow sponge printing. **No mark.** £60, $120.

Center right: 832. Plate. 8.25" (20.9 cm). Six brown lines. An outer ring of green motifs and two inner bands of red. **No mark.** £50, $100.

Bottom right: 833. Bowl with beaded everted rim. 9.25" (23.5 cm). Two narrow yellow bands enclose two broad green bands which in turn enclose a band of red sponge printing. **No mark.** £55, $110.

Top left: 834. Soup plate. 7.125″ (18.1 cm). Red lines. The outer sponged band is brown; the inner band is blue/green. **No mark.** £30, $60.

Top right: 835. Plate. 8.625″ (21.9 cm). A flow blue border also found in the GEM pattern. **No mark.** £30, $60.

Center left: 836. Bowl. 13.25″ (33.7 cm). This may be a washbowl from a bedroom set or an Irish Potato Bowl. It is hard to decide which from the photograph. It was bought with 807 as a pair but they do not match. Blue motifs. **No mark.** £70, $140.

Center right: 837. Saucer. A green band between blue lines. The band is overprinted with black sponge printed motifs. **No mark.** £55, $110.

Bottom right: 838. Saucer. Similar to the above. A broad blue band with overprinted black flowers lies between green lines. Both saucers are very deep. **No mark.** £45, $90.

Top left: 839. Bowl. 8.5″ (21.6 cm). Red and green sponged triangles between blue lines. This is certainly a late piece, made in the twentieth century. **No mark.** £30, $60.

Top right: 840. Plate. 9″ (22.9 cm). Two bands of green motifs and red lines. **No mark.** £55, $110.

Center left: 841. Mug. 3.125″ (7.9 cm). The lines are blue and the sponged "eyes" are brown. **No mark.** £55, $110.

Center right: 842. Cup. A pale blue line with green and crimson sponged motifs. **No mark.** £60, $120.

Bottom right: 843. Cup and saucer. Blue motifs. **No mark.** £70, $140.

Top left: 844. Cup and saucer. Red motifs. **No mark.** These last two show how basic sponge printing could be. In the quest for keeping costs down, decoration was kept to a minimum, though not necessarily carelessly done. £65, $130.

Top right: 845. Cup and saucer. The bows are purple with one on the bottom of the interior. A loosely textured sponge was used. **No mark.** £40, $80.

Center left: 846. Cup and saucer. Blue lines with a complex sponge in red, green and brown. Very skilful printing. **No mark.** £65, $130.

Center right: 847. Slop basin, bread plate from a child's set. The sponged motifs are blue and are reminiscent of known Clyde Pottery pieces. **No mark.** £55, $110.

Bottom right: 848. Cup and saucer. Green line with red motifs. **No mark.** £45, $90.

Left to right, top to bottom:
849. Cup and saucer. Green lines with blue diamond motifs. **No mark.** £40, $80.

850. Child's cup and saucer. Red leaf motifs. **No mark.** £30, $60.

851. Child's cup and saucer. Red leaf sponged motifs but smaller than in the above piece. **No mark.** £30, $60.

852. Child's cup and saucer. Black flowers and leaves alternate with yellow dots. It is also known in red and green. **No mark.** £70, $140.

853. Cup and saucer. All in purple. **No mark.** £35, $70.

854. Cup. 3.5" (8.9 cm). Red lines and paired green leaves. **No mark.** £55, $110.

Left to right, top to bottom:
855. Cup and saucer. Red ovals joined by green arcs. **No mark.** £25, $50.

856. Cup. Green lines and blue sponged motifs. **No mark.** £50, $100.

857. Plate. 8.5" (21.6 cm). Blue lines and red sponged motifs. **No mark.** £35, $70.

858. Child's saucer. 4.5" (11.4 cm). Blue motif. **No mark.** £50, $100.

859. Child's cup and saucer. Red lines, green motifs with red central dots. **No mark.** £70, $140.

860. Bowl. Dark green throughout. **No mark.** £40, $80.

Top left: 861. Mug. 3.25″ (8.3 cm). Red lines and a deep blue sponge print. **No mark.** £70, $140.

Top right: 862. Cream jug. 2.75″ (6.9 cm). Sponged motifs in green. **No mark.** £70, $140.

Center left: 863. Mug. 3.625″ (9 cm). A broad band of blue and narrower bands of pink and brown with Maltese crosses overprinted in black. Black lining at the top and the bottom. **No mark.** £70, $140.

Center right: 864. Child's tureen. 2.5″ high (6.3 cm). Molded with daisies. Red lines and green Maltese crosses. **No mark.** £100, $200.

Bottom center: 865. Razor box. 8.375″ (21 cm). Blue motifs. **No mark.** £75, $150.

Top left: 866. Pitcher. 3.5" high (8.9 cm). Sponge printed in blue. It has the same shape as 868. **No mark.** £100, $200.

Top right: 867. Ewer. 11" (27.9 cm). Sponge printed in purple. The rim motif occurs both inside and outside, a most unusual feature. It is very light in weight. **No mark.** £50, $100.

Center left: 868. Pitcher. 3.5" (8.9 cm). The top motif is brown, the central one blue. This is exactly the size and shape of 866. **No mark.** £40, $80.

Center right: 869. Child's teapot. 4.5" high (11.4 cm). Red lines and light blue sponged motifs. **No mark.** £90, $180.

Bottom right: 870. Sugar basin. 4" high (10.2 cm). All decoration in light blue. **No mark.** £70, $140.

Top left: 871. Sugar basin. 4.125″ high (10.5 cm). Blue daisies with red centers. **No mark.** £30, $60.

Top right: 872. Child's teapot. 4″ high (10.2 cm). Durrie's **"Snowflake." No mark.** £75, $150.

Center left: 873. Sauceboat and underplate. Decorated in blue. **No mark.** £60, $120.

Center right: 874. Cup. A red band with black leaves. The lower and inner lines are blue. **No mark.** £65, $130.

Bottom right: 875. Plate. 9″ (22.9 cm). All the decoration is red. **No mark.** £60, $120.

Top left: 876. Plate. 8.36" (21.6 cm). Brown lines. The outer sponged motifs are green, the inner ones red. **No mark.** £40, $80.

Top right: 877. Plate. 8.625" (21.9 cm). A green rim line and three light lines in red with alternate green circles and blue flowers. **No mark.** £70, $140.

Center left: 878. Small plate. 3" (7.6 cm). All in blue. **No mark.** Perhaps from a child's tea set. £75, $150.

Center right: 879. Saucer. 5.875" (14.9 cm). Green leaves and shapes with cutout floral centers; red shapes with superimposed yellow motifs. **No mark.** £40, $80.

Bottom right: 880. Cup and saucer. Blue lines, red bows and green daisies. A loosely textured sponge. **No mark.** £70, $140.

Top left: 881. Bowl. 9.75" (25.3 cm). Decorated internally with deep blue motifs. It has molded spirals. **No mark.** £45, $90.

Top right: 882. Soup plate. 7.875" (20 cm). Decorated entirely in brown. **No mark.** £35, $70.

Center left: 883. Plate. 8.75" (22 cm). Yellow bows and red daisies with blue lines. A loosely textured sponge. **No mark.** £70, $140.

Center right: 884. Child's cup and saucer. Black lines, red sponged Maltese crosses and green dots. **No mark.** £65, $130.

Bottom right: 885. Cup. 4.375" (11.1 cm). Blue lines on body and handle. A red sponge print. **No mark.** £40, $80.

Top left: 886. Rice dish. 9" (22.9 cm). Green lines, red lattice motif and green leaves. There is an indistinct impressed mark. £30, $60.

Top right: 887. Cup. A red line and red bells hanging from a leafy band. **No mark.** £40, $80.

Center left: 888. Plate. c. 4" (10.2 cm). Decorated in blue. **No mark.** £30, $60.

Center right: 889. Saucer. A blue line and red sponged motifs. An indecipherable impressed mark. £30, $60.

Bottom right: 890. Child's saucer. The outer ring is a red sponge print on a red line. The inner ring has green crosses. **No mark.** £40, $80.

Top left: 891. Cup and saucer. Pale blue decoration. **No mark.** £30, $60.

Top right: 892. Cup and saucer. Red decoration. **No mark.** £45, $90.

Center left: 893. Teapot stand. Green decoration. **No mark.** £25, $50.

Center right: 894. Soup plate. 10" (25.4 cm). Shades of brown. This is the famous **GRECIAN** pattern, more usual in gray and made by many potteries both known and unknown in Scotland and England. The pattern dates from after 1875. **No mark.** £80, $160.

Bottom right: 895. Saucer. Green lines and inner band of decoration. Between these are red motifs. **No mark.** £30, $60.

Top left: 896. Saucer. Arched black lines with alternating red and green leaves. **No mark.** £30, $60.

Top right: 897. Soup plate. Flow blue in three separate sponge prints. **No mark.** Sponge printing in flow blue is relatively scarce. £70, $140.

Center left: 898. Cup and saucer. Green lines and the outer sponged band; the inner band is red. **No mark.** £45, $90.

Center right: 899. Saucer. A red line and blue sponge printed motifs. **No mark.** £75, $150.

Bottom right: 900. Cup and saucer. Black lines, red bows and green flowers. **No mark.** £45, $90.

Top left: 901. Mug. 3.75" (9.5 cm). A broad green band, a black line, and red sponge printed motifs. **No mark.** £75, $150.

Top right: 902. Soup plate. 9.5" (24.1 cm). Closely-packed sponged motifs in flow blue. **No mark.** £90, $180.

Center left: 903. Plate. 6.375" (16.2 cm). Very light in weight and decorated entirely in blue. **No mark.** £80, $160.

Center right: 904. Child's sugar basin with four feet. All decoration in dark green. **No mark.** £80, $160.

Bottom right: 905. Plate. 8.375" (21.3 cm). A red border and leaves in the same as well as brown and green. Finlayson attributes a similar plate to the Links Pottery of Kirkcaldy but it is dangerous to attribute on the grounds of one motif. **No mark.** £95, $190.

Top left: 906. Bowl. 8.375" (21.3 cm). A red line and an outer band of deep blue. A red inner line and flares. Between are green motifs. Bought in England. **No mark.** £40, $80.

Top right: 907. Dish. 9.25" (23.5 cm), flange 1.375" (3.5 cm). The flange has red and yellow flowers and green leaves. The rest is light blue. A red rim line. **No mark.** £35, $70.

Center left: 908. Plate. 8.625" (21.9 cm). An overall pattern. **No mark.** £75, $150.

Center right: 909. Plate. 9" (22.9 cm). A band of almost Greek key in red. The middle band is blue and the inner green. **No mark.** £40, $80.

Bottom right: 910. Cup and saucer. Blue lines flank green flowers. **No mark.** £75, $150.

Top left: 911. Bowl. 10.5" (26.7 cm). Leaves in blue and flowers in lighter blue. **No mark.** £95, $190.

Top right: 912. Sugar basin. 5.5" x 4.5" (14 x 11.4 cm). Vertical rows of red diamonds alternate with green stars, both in a loose texture of sponge. **No mark.** £100, $200.

Center left: 913. Bowl with beaded rim. 8.5" (21.6 cm). Overall red and blue motifs and green diamonds throughout. **No mark.** £30, $60.

Center right: 914. Platter or ashet. 11.865 x 8.625" (30.1 x 21.9 cm). Lines from outer to inner are blue, blue, blue, and yellow. Between the first two is a broad yellow band with red sponged motifs. The inner band of motifs is green. **No mark.** £30, $60.

Bottom right: 915. Bowl with beaded rim. 11" (27.9 cm). Three broad red bands. The outer and innermost bands of sponge printing are blue. The middle one is green. **No mark.** £50, $100.

Top left: 916. Plate. 9.25" (23.5 cm). Brown leaves alternate with blue motifs. **No mark.** £100, $200.

Top right: 917. Cup and saucer. Red lines and a band of green which has black sponge printed motifs on it. **No mark.** £45, $90.

Center left: 918. Dish. 5.75" (14.6 cm). A green rim band. The center and inner bands are red with overprinted yellow "snowflakes." **No mark.** £120, $240.

Center right: 919. Irish Potato Bowl or Washbowl. 12.5" (31.8 cm). One blue cut sponge only used, even the rim has a half-print from it. **No mark.** £120, $240.

Bottom right: 920. Mug with two handles. 4" (10.2 cm). A blue sponge print inside and outside on the rim. **No mark.** £40, $80.

Left to right, top to bottom: 921 and 922. Treacle (molasses) jug with lid. 6" (15.2 cm). The lid threads into the body, a technique much more common in stoneware. Sponge printed in blue. The use and the shape would both suggest an American origin. **No mark.** £70, $140.

923. Bowl. 5.625" (14.3 cm). Very dark and uncontrolled flow blue with two rows of motifs. Perhaps Scottish. **No mark.** £75, $150.

924. Plate. 8.75" (22 cm). A pale green rim line and red border sponging with a smaller version in the center. Between is a painted element of green leaves with blue sponged dot flowers. **No mark.** £110, $220.

925. Plate. 8.625" (21.9 cm). Blue lines enclose red sponged motifs separated by green lines. The central motifs are yellow and green. **No mark.** £90, $180.

926. Molded leaf dish. 11.25 x 8.375" (28.6 x 21.3 cm). The molded dragonfly is painted blue, matching the sponged border. Another recorded specimen has no paint on the dragonfly but sponge printed birds. **No mark.** £80, $160.

Left to right, top to bottom:

927. Soup plate or rice dish. 9" (22.9 cm). Red lines outline the blue sponged flange band. The diamond shapes are blue and the next band green. The central yellow and purple flower is also painted. The border is very like that found on **GARDEN**. Perhaps also an "Asian" piece. **No mark.** £95, $190.

928. Plate. 8.75" (22 cm). Blue lines enclose a red sponged border. The painted center has blue swags enclosing a yellow space. Swags join at red and green leaves; the central motifs are blue. **No mark.** £110, $220.

929. Plaque. 9.25" (23.5 cm). Punctured at the top for hanging. A molded classical figure with cornucopia and red painted robes. Red line and blue sponged border. **No mark.** £110, $220.

930. Plate. 8" (20.3 cm). Sponge printed blue/green crosses. A central transfer of a tea party with **LADIES ALL PRAY MAKE FREE AND TELL ME HOW YOU LIKE YOUR TEA**. **No mark.** £85, $170.

931. Plate. 6.9" (17.7 cm). A blue sponge printed border. The central scene is one of a series of transfer prints called **BAND OF HOPE** - this one is **SIGNING THE PLEDGE**. **No mark.** £85, $170.

932. Plate. 5.375" (13.7 cm). Another **BAND OF HOPE** plate - **THE SABBATH KEEPERS. RISE EARLY AND THANKFULLY PUT UP YOUR PRAYER. BE AT SCHOOL IN GOOD TIME AND BE DILIGENT THERE.** A blue sponge printed border. **No mark.** £85, $170.

933. Plate. 7" (17.8 cm). The sponge printed border is red. The central print of three Oriental boys teasing a goat - one riding it, one twisting its tail and one holding a mirror up to it. **No mark.** £80, $160.

934. Platter or ashet. 12.75 x 9.5" (32.4 x 24.1 cm). Small green central transfer print and yellow sponge printed border. **No mark.** £85, $170.

935. Plate. 9.5" (24.1 cm). Blue sponge printed edging. A black transfer print - **CUTTING THE WHEAT**. An illegible mark. £100, $200.

Center right: 936. Plate. 7.125" (18.1 cm). Sponge printed brown edging. The transfer print is brown and clobbered in red, green, blue and yellow. **No mark.** £50, $100.

Bottom right: 937. Plate. 6.375" (16.2 cm). A heavily molded border with sponge printed flowers and green leaves. A central green transfer print **GATHERING FLOWERS**. **No mark.** £30, $60.

938. Bowl. 8.5″ (21.6 cm). A blue sponge printed border and a brown transfer print of **Little Red Riding Hood and the Wolf** with sponged or dabbed green grass. **No mark.** £55, $110.

939. Saucer. 4.5″ (11.4 cm). Brown sponge printed motifs exist in a network of blue and red dabbing. **No mark.** £60, $120.

940. Plate. c. 8″ (20.3 cm). A dark brown line runs close by a simple motif in mauve round the rim. **No mark.** Collection: Hunterian Museum, University of Glasgow. £30, $60.

941. Pitcher. c. 6″ (15.2 cm). All in dark purple. Bands of Maltese crosses within circles run round the rim and the base; the belly shows a band of a vaguely leafy motif. **No mark.** Collection: Hunterian Museum, University of Glasgow. £60, $120.

942. Two mugs. c. 4″ (10.2 cm). Each has two black lines and is decorated in crimson and blue, one with a double cable motif. **No mark**s. Collection: Hunterian Museum, University of Glasgow. £80, $160.

943. Soup plate. c. 8.5" (21.6 cm). Two blue lines. The flange has a cross-like motif in brown. A tiny blue motif occurs between each pair of brown motifs and also within the center of each. **No mark.** Collection: Hunterian Museum, University of Glasgow. £80, $160.

944. Bowl. Two motifs, one in green, one in red, alternate in slanting vertical rows of three. **No mark.** £50, $100.

945. Bowl with beaded rim. Two bands of yellow are bounded by black lines and have superimposed black sponged motifs. Between is a black sponged Greek key pattern. **No mark.** £90, $180.

946. Bowl. c. 9" (22.9 cm). Five black lines. The first two enclose a yellow band. Then we have a pink band with superimposed black sponged motif. Below are two thinner green bands. **No mark.** Collection: Hunterian Museum, University of Glasgow. £65, $130.

947. Mug. Between two olive lines is a wide pink band on which are superimposed black starlike motifs. **No mark.** £60, $120.

948. Detail of bowl. A row of red diamonds at the rim is echoed at the base. Between is a band of leaves of unusual complexity since each is colored in red, green and brown. **No mark.** £35, $70.

949. Covered bowl with two handles. c. 7″ (17.8 cm). Most of the exterior is covered in pink and the lid and body each have one band of green leaves with gold painting. **No mark.** Collection: Hunterian Museum, University of Glasgow. £30, $60.

950. Invalid spit pot. c. 4″ (10.2 cm). A single row of orange diamonds decorates the interior and the exterior of the rim. Below is a very unusual combination of what appears to be orange leaves superimposed on gray leaves. **No mark.** £40, $80.

951. Plate. c. 8″ (20.3 cm). **GRECIAN** in an unfamiliar blue color instead of the usual gray. **No mark.** Collection: Hunterian Museum, University of Glasgow. £130, $260.

952. Plate. c. 8″ (20.3 cm). All in gray/green. A row of fans decorates the flange, then a line encloses a simple decoration of a starlike sponge in the well. **No mark.** Kingussie, the Highland Folk Museum, Highland Council. £75, $150.

953. Soup plate. c. 8″ (20.3 cm). A crimson line at the rim and a band of blue abstract motifs on the flange are the only decoration. **No mark.** Collection: Hunterian Museum, University of Glasgow. £110, $220.

954. Pitcher. The rim has a band of blue motifs. The belly of the piece is covered with stripes of crimson, yellow and green with a superimposed black sponged motif. The handle has a crimson stripe. **No mark.** £85, $170.

955. Pitcher. All sponged in purple. A band decorates the rim while two rebands of one motif reversed decorate the belly. **No mark.** £50, $100.

956. Pitcher. c. 8″ (20.3 cm). A band of crimson abstract motifs at the rim. Two black lines on the body are bounded by bands of blue motifs on the exterior. Between them are vertical lines of green crosses with crimson feather motifs between. **No mark.** £75, $150.

957. Mug. c. 5″ (12.7 cm). Bands of blue crosses at rim and base. The middle of the exterior has a band of interlinked, reversed S's in gray. **No mark.** £45, $90.

958. Bowl. c. 6″ (15.2 cm). Two black lines enclose a band of pink "leaves." **No mark.** Collection: Kingussie, the Highland Folk Museum, Highland Council. £40, $80.

959. Bowl. c. 5" (12.7 cm). The bowl has a slight carination towards the base which is found on many Scottish bowls. Dabbed, vertical, crimson stripes separate vertical groups of three squares with dots in green. **No mark.** Collection: Kingussie, the Highland folk Museum, Highland Council. £40, $80.

960. Bowl. Two yellow lines enclose a band of gray leaflike motifs. **No mark.** Collection: Kingussie, the Highland Folk Museum, Highland Council. £35, $70.

961. Bowl. All in blue. Two double lines enclose a row of "leaves." **No mark.** Collection: Kingussie, the Highland Folk Museum, Highland Council. £45, $90.

962. Bowl. c. 7" (17.8 cm). A double gray line at the rim and a band of gray botanical motifs are the only decoration. **No mark.** £70, $140.

963. Bowl. A blue rim line touches a row of fringed "eyes" in brown. This fringed motif is found on a large number of pieces which can be attributed to Clyde Pottery in Greenock which had a large export trade with Ireland where this bowl was found. The owners of Clyde Pottery also briefly owned a pottery at Larne. **No mark.** Collection: Ulster Folk and Transport Museum, NMGNI. £65, $130.

964. Bowl. c. 5.5" (14 cm). Three motifs form a band round the rim. A green diamond, a pink oval (perhaps meant as a double chain) and a brown "star" or "flower." This is undoubtedly the most carelessly decorated bowl yet recorded; yet it was passed and sold, perhaps as a second. **No mark.** Collection: Hunterian Museum, University of Glasgow. £100, $200.

965. Mug. 2.6" high (6.6 cm). A band of crimson "weavers' combs" runs, somewhat unsteadily, round the rim. This mug has also been recorded in green instead of crimson. **No mark.** £90, $180.

966. c. 4" (10.2 cm). Two shades of purple, the darker motif above. Both motifs are obviously based on plant forms. **No mark.** £90, $180.

967. Mug. A red/brown stripe at the rim is echoed in a complex motif on each side in red/brown and black, showing a flag with a C. This piece was almost certainly made for a shipping line. **No mark.** Collection: Ulster Folk and Transport Museum, NMGNI. £70, $140.

Left: 968. Mug. All in sepia. A double cable rim surmounts a set of fleurs-de-lis on each side. **No mark.** Collection: Ulster Folk and Transport Museum, NMGNI. £70, $140.

Right: 969. Mug. A crimson stripe at the rim surmounts a complex motif of a brown wreath round a blue crown on each side. **No mark.** Collection: Ulster Folk and Transport Museum, NMGNI. £120, $240.

970. Bowl. There are two rows of alternating green shamrocks and red crosses with dots. **No mark.** £40, $80.

971. Bowl. A rim band of pink "acanthus" surmounts blue fleurs-de-lis laid on their side. **No mark.** £80, $160.

972. Bowl. c. 8" (20.3 cm). Two black lines enclose a blue motif like roof tiling. Below this are crimson, yellow and black motifs. **No mark.** £45, $90.

973. Bowl. A crimson rim line is the only decoration apart from a band of black "eyes" with dots. **No mark.** Collection: Kingussie, the Highland Folk Museum, Highland Council. £90, $180.

974. Bowl with beaded rim. 9.25″ (23.5 cm). Three crimson lines of varying thickness. The first and second enclose a three deep chess board of green, yellow and uncoloured squares. These have alternative overprints of black stars and five dots with Hs. **No mark.** £70, $140.

975. Cup and saucer. A crimson line is the only decoration inside the cup. The exterior and the saucer each have a row of dark green sponge printing. **No mark.** £60, $120.

976. Bowl. Black lines enclose purple dabbing over which are sponge printed shamrocks. The shape of bowl was widely made in Scotland, most prolifically by the Victoria Pottery, Pollockshaws, which is now part of Glasgow. **No mark.** £80, $160.

977. Soup plate. c. 7.5" (19 cm). Blue lines round the rim enclose a band of black Greek key, four motifs of which appear also superimposed on a crimson disc in the center. Between these is a band of black sponge printed leaves. **No mark.** £75, $150.

978. Plate. c. 8" (20.5 cm). A variant of **GARDEN** with crimson and blue sponge printing, and crimson, green and yellow painting. **No mark.** £60, $120.

979. Plate. c. 8" (20.5 cm). Very early looking sponge printing in blue overall. There is an indecipherable impressed mark. £60, $120.

980. Plate. c. 8" (20.5 cm). A very carefully sponge printed plate divided by three painted lines in crimson, purple and green. These separate different motifs in dark blue, light blue and green. There is a central flower in purple and yellow. **No mark.** £120, $240.

981. Rice dish. c. 8" (20.5 cm). There is a heavy blue motif round the rim and a central area covered by four motifs of a lilac "flower" with green leaves. In the very center of the well is a double blue circle. As if the "flower" were not odd enough, there is a heavy blue cross painted on top of all of this which is so far unique, so it is included although damaged. **No mark.** £100, $200.

982 and 983. A recently discovered plate. c. 8" (20.5 cm). It is so far unique in that it is both marked and dated. A carelessly printed border in brown surrounds four multicolored thistle prints and the painted legend D.G.G. 1881 in the same colors. The mark probably refers to the Britannia Pottery, Glasgow, rather than the same city's Verreville Pottery. Both were operated by the same family and used this pottery description at this time but the style seems nearer to Britannia. £150, $300.

Index of Spongeware Potters

American

Mayer, (J. & E.) Potteries Co., Ltd.
Morris, W. T. & Filmore, F. R.
Sebring Pottery Co.
Willets Manufacturing Co.

British

Adams, William & Son(s)
Adams, W. & T.
Adderleys Ltd.
Allerton, Charles & Sons (Ltd.)
Aynsley, H. & Co. (Ltd.)
Baker (W.) & Co. (Ltd.)
Balfour, Alexander & Co.
Barlow, T. W. & Son, Ltd.
Bell, J. & M. P. (& Co.) (Ltd.)
Belleek & Co.
Booth, Thomas & Son
Britannia Pott. Co. Ltd.
British Anchor Pottery Co. Ltd.
Caledonian Pottery
Campbellfield Pottery Co. (Ltd.)
Clementson Bros. (Ltd.)
Clyde Pottery Co. (Ltd.)
Cochran & Fleming
- Britannia Pottery
Cochran, R. & Co.
- Verreville Pottery
Davenport
Edge, Malkin & Co. (Ltd.)
Elsmore & Forster
Green, T. G. & Co. (Ltd.)
Hammersley, Ralph (& Son(s))
Harvey, C. & W. K.
- noted as Charles Harvey & Sons
Heron, Robert (& Son)
Jamieson, James & Co.
Jones, George (& Sons, Ltd.)
Kidston, R. A. & Co.
Lockhart & Arthur
Lockhart, David (& Co.)
Lockhart, David & Sons
McNay, C. W. (& Sons)
Marshall, John (& Co.) (Ltd.)
Meakin & Co.
- noted as Meakin Bros. & Co.
Meakin, J. & G. (Ltd.)
Methven, David & Sons
Nautilus Porcelain Co.
Possil Pottery
Powell & Bishop
Price Bros. (Burslem) Ltd.
Rathbone, T. & Co.
Reeves, James
Reid, William (& Son(s))
Shirley, Thomas & Co.
South Wales Potters
Thompson, John (& Sons)
Watson & Co.
Unidentified

European

Amberg, Adolph (Modler)
Annaburg Steingutfabrik, A. G.
Boch Frères
Establissments Cêramiques de St. Amand-Les-Eaux
Faience et Porcelaines de Saint Amand et Hamage
Ginori, Richard
Keller & Guerin, Kuznietsoff
Mouzin Lecat & Co.
Nouvelles Usines Cêramiques du Nord, S. A.
Onnaing Nord F.
Petrus Regout (& Co.)
St. Clement
Société Cêramique
Utzschneider/Sarreguemines
Villeroy & Boch
Wilhelmsburg
Unidentified

Annotated Bibliography

The following books (excluding listed encyclopedias) are written partly or wholly on spongeware. They are referred to in the text by the author's surname, with or without a date.

Baumann 1991.—*Collecting Antique Marbles* by Paul Baumann. 2nd edition, Wallace-Homestead Book Co., Radnor Pennsylvania, 1991.

Mainly about glass marbles but there is a chapter on carpet bowls with much misleading information and some good illustrations.

Bell & Gillan—*The Potteries of Tyneside* by R.C. Bell and M.A.V. Gillan. Newcastle, 1973.

A survey of Newcastle potteries.

Bell, Dixon & Cottle—*Maling, a Tyneside Pottery* by Bell, Dixon & Cottle. Newcastle, 1987.

Maling made spongeware.

Collard—*Nineteenth Century Pottery and Porcelain in Canada* by Elizabeth Collard. McGill-Queen's University Press. Kingston and Montreal, 1967. 2nd edition, 1984.

This book is clearly thought out and expressed and conveys an immense amount of information, a little of it on spongeware.

Cruickshank—*Scottish Spongeware* by Graeme Cruickshank. Scottish Pottery Studies 1. Edinburgh, 1982.

An excellent small volume whose only real fault is a parochialism which leads to some very suspect attributions.

Danckert – *Directory of European Porcelain* by Ludwig Danckert. N. A. G. Press, Ltd., London, England, 1992.

Illustrates marks and photographs of spongeware.

Davis & Rankine—*Wemyss Ware* by P. Davis and Robert Rankine. Scottish Academic Press, Edinburgh and London, 1986.

Provides a price list for spongeware exported to Ireland by the Fife Pottery.

Finlayson—*Portneuf Pottery and Other Early Wares* by R.W. Finlayson. Longman, Ontario, Canada, 1972.

This book is full of very beautiful color photographs of spongeware and equally full of hard and accurate information, putting paid forever to the idea that Portneauf Pottery is an entity in itself. It is simply the spongeware imported to Canada from Britain.

Fleming 1923—*Scottish Pottery* by J. Arnold Fleming – Glasgow. Maclehose, Jackson & Co., 1923.

This is a seminal work on spongeware as on so many other subjects but is well known for inaccuracies in detail.

Furniss & Wagners—*Adams Ceramics* by David A. Furniss, J. Richard Wagner & Judith Wagner. Schiffer Publishing Ltd., Atglen, Pennsylvania, 1999.

Very informative on Adams spongeware but a whole book could be written on that subject.

Godden—*Encyclopaedia of British Pottery and Porcelain Marks* by Geoffrey A. Godden. Barrie & Jenkins, London, revised 1993.

Selected Godden marks from the above encyclopaedia are referenced as **GDN**.

Greaser—*Homespun Ceramics* by Arlene & Paul Greaser. Wallace-Homestead Book Co. Des Moines, Iowa.

This work contains many pictures in black and white but what they are meant to be pictures of is enigmatic. Spatterware, spongeware, delft, dabbed ware, brushstroke and other things are all confused — a confusion that is echoed in the text. "Soft paste creamware" is particularly mysterious.

Hughes & Pugh—*Llanelly Pottery* by Gareth Hughes and Robert Pugh. Llanelli Borough Council, Llanelli, 1990.

Provides information on spongeware manufacture in Wales. An earlier book on the same subject is Llanelly Pottery by Dilys Jenkins - Swansea 1968. Unfortunately she practically ignores the production of spongeware.

Jewitt— *The Ceramic Art of Great Britain* by Llewellyn Jewitt (new rev. edition) New Orchard Editions, London, 1985.

An essential work for any research into British ceramics. Many makers of spongeware are mentioned.

Kowalsky – *Encyclopedia of Marks on American, English & European Earthenware, Ironstone, & Stoneware, 1780-1980* by Arnold & Dorothy Kowalsky, Schiffer Publishing, Ltd., Atglen, Pennsylvania, 1999.

Provides a selection of marks found on spatterware, spongeware, brushstroke, as well as information on the various potters. Selected Kowalsky marks from the above encyclopedia are referenced as **KAD**.

Kelly 1993—*Scottish Sponge-Printed Pottery* by Henry E. Kelly. Lomondside Press, Glasgow, Scotland, 1993.

The latest publication which tried to sum up our knowledge of spongeware at the time. The color plates are very useful but there are one of two reversals in captions.

Kelly 1999—*Scottish Ceramics* by Henry E. Kelly. Schiffer Publishing, Ltd., Atglen, Pennsylvania, 1999.

Illustrates several different types of spongeware, particularly those of Scottish origin.

Ketchum—*American Country Pottery, Yellowware, Spongeware* by William C. Ketchum. Alfred A. Knopf, New York, 1987.

An excellent book which provides the names of quite a few American spongeware manufacturers.

King—*Photographs of Victoria Pottery, Pollokshaws* with comment by Elspeth King in Scottish Pottery Historical Review 12 1988/9.

In several of these posed photographs spongeware is evident. In one there is a whole warehouse full of it! The original album of photographs is kept in the People's Palace in Glasgow.

Papers which appeared in the publications of the Scottish Pottery Society (The Scottish Pottery Historical Review [SPHR] is the journal of the Scottish Pottery Society.) Full reference to all of these will be found in Kelly 1993.

McConnell—*Spatterware and Spongeware* by Kevin McConnell. Schiffer Publishing Ltd., Atglen, Pennsylvania, 1990.

'Full of excellent color plates. The spongeware illustrated, however, is almost all of a very primitive type providing no idea of the scope of the technique.

McGovern—*Interview with Mrs. McGovern* in Scottish Pottery (a journal) Vol. 1, No. 1 - Glasgow, 1978.

Mrs. McGovern had actually printed spongeware at Verreville Pottery as a girl. This is reprinted as Appendix 1 in this volume.

Penkala – *European Pottery, A Guide for the Collector and Dealer* by Maria Penkala, F.R.G.S. Interbook International B.V., Ssciedam, The Netherlands, 1980.

Illustrates marks and photographs of spongeware.

Polling –*Maastrichtse Ceramiek, Merken en Dateringen, P. Regout, (De Sphinx), N.A. Bosch, Clermont en Chainaye, Société Céramique, Guillaume Lambert, L. Regout (Mosa), F. Regout, Alfred Regout (Rema)* by A. Polling. Utigeversmaatschappij Antiek, The Netherlands, 1993.

Illustrates marks and photographs of spongeware.

Robacker—*Spatterware and Sponge, Hardy Perennials of Ceramics* by Earl F. & Ada F. Robacker. Cranbury, New Jersey. A.S. Barnes & Co., Inc., 1979.

A book greatly prized in the U.S.A. and virtually unknown elsewhere. It is an immense advance on 'Homespun Ceramics' but has fixed the strange vocabulary used by dealers in the U.S.A.

Rontgen –*Marks on German, Bohemian & Austrian Porcelain, 1710 to the Present* by Robert E. Rontgen. Schiffer Publishing Ltd., Atglen, Pennsylvania, 1981 and Lochem b.v., Germany, 1993.

Illustrates marks and photographs of spongeware

Slesin et al.—*Kitchen Ceramics* by Suzanne Slesin, Daniel Rozensztroch & Stafford Cliff. Abbeville Press Publishers, New York, 1997.

A book that confuses spongeware, dabbed ware, spatterware and splash glazes, and also provides very little information but has the most beautiful pictures since Finlayson's *Portneuf Pottery*.

Sunderland — *Sunderland Pottery*, Anon. Tyne & Wear County Council Museums, Sunderland, 1984.

A comprehensive survey of Sunderland potteries. Many mentions of spongeware.

Tettoni et al.—*Myanmar Style* by Luca Invernizzi Tettoni, et al. Thames & Hudson, London, England.

It has two pages on foreign ceramics with a breathtaking glimpse of a large collection of export spongeware.

Turner—*William Adams, an Old English Potter* by William Turner, London, 1904.

Asserts that spongeware was taught to English potters by imported Scots. An essential tool in research, stronger on English than on Scottish marks.

V&B—Villeroy & Boch 1748-1930, an Exhibition Catalogue. Rijksmuseum, Amsterdam, 1977.

One illustration looks like a sponge-printed piece; otherwise the subject is ignored, which is typical of the attitude of many potteries.

Appendix

These extracts, from a taped interview made in December 1976, were first published in January 1978 in a bulletin of the Glasgow Branch of the Scottish Pottery Society called "Scottish Pottery." Mrs. B. McGovern, aged 83 in 1976, had worked as a girl in Verreville Pottery in Finnieston Street in Glasgow, c. 1913-16. She had ended as a paintress but had begun, as did many others, in the spongeware department. The interview is in the form of questions and answers and the transcriber (Tony Henry) has tried to indicate Mrs. McGovern's accent.

Q. Go back to the time you started - your first day in the pottery - and tell me what the place looked like.

A. We startit at half past six in the mornin. We got a brek from 9 to 10 o'cloak fur wur brekfast, then we startit agin at 10 till half past one. We had wur dinner, and worked right to six o'cloak.

Q. Did you work Saturday morning also?

A. Saturday mornin an a. Fae nine tae twelve.

Q. When you started in the pottery, where did you go the first day?

A. Well, ah canna mind that... ye went intae the spongin shoap an ye goat a joab there...Ah wis wan o the penters, but we werna that at the time. Ye didna get yir joab right away...ye tried what ye could dae. Ah helped the spongers. After that ye got yer joab as a penter. The next room wis the printin place - it wis nearly a men that worked in that, at printin. There wis a gildin shoap where they did the dishes gold - roond aboot the rim. Some printin was done in gold.

Q. They PRINTED it in gold?

A. Aye, they printit it in gold. The likes o that wee cup ye see there, there woould be a flower on that and the gold roon it.

Q. And the man would paint that in would he?

A. Aye, he would paint that in.

Q. And what sort of things were they making? Mainly dinner sets and tea sets?

A. Aye.

Q. For spongeware, you cut a pattern out on the sponge and dabbed it on?

A. Aye, that's right. And some o it was hand-paintit. A part o the shoap was for hand paintin. That's the bit we were in.

Q. Did they make anything like pottery jugs?

A. Oh yes. Further doon, that's where they made a the moulds. They made jougs, cups an saucers, plates. We collectit them, took them up tae oor shoap and hand-paintit or sponged them.

Q. And can you remember any of the names of the people there, who the boss was? You mentioned it was Mr. Cochran's pottery. Was he there when you were there?

A. Oh aye. He was the heid yin. He was the heid wan. He wald come in an hae a walk roon just tae see hoo things were goan oan.

Q. You said your brother also worked there.

A. Aye, Paddy (Goad rest him). And Willie worked in it for a while. Paddy was a kilnman. He carrit the stuff - like the men took the stuff oan boards, an put it into the kiln fur tae fire it up and tae bring it oot tae get it paintit or sponged or the like o that. It was taken tae the dip hoose and was putt intae a big byne and dippit in there. An it can oot. An they fired it, and it cam oot glossy.

Q. And that was the only job he worked at?

A. Aye. Paddy was a kilnman.

Q. Was there any other members of the family worked in the pottery?

A. Naw - jist me and Paddy and Willie.

Q. And what did Willia do?

A. Willie wis in anither joab - carryin the stuff doon tae the kiln tae get it fired up. Paddy was the foreman.

Q. Can you remember anything about the wages you earned there? Your wages?

A. Well, when ah startit first ah goat 5 shillings a week. An them ah wis pit on piecework. It's whatever yourself made, ye got yer pai fur it.

Q. And can you remember how much the rate was, per piece or cup?

A. Oh no, ye didna get paid that way - ye goat payed when the joab wis finished. Say ah wis daen a loat o plates, well if ah did 2 dozen, that went doon in ma book.

Q. Can you remember what happened to the faulty pieces?

A. We jist fling them oot. A van came and took them away.

Q. A horse and cart?

A. Aye. Then there was the place where they made the dishes. They had a mould, the same as a bowl they were makin and they pit it oan - what wid ye call it? - a wee thingammy that whirled roon - a wheel. If it wasnae right they jist whupped it oot.

Q. Was that separate from where you were working?

A. Aye. Then it was sent up tae the dip hoose where it was dipped and fired. Paddy's crowd took it and fired it. They were putt in for mebbe a couple o nights and there were a man there tae watch, shovellin in the coal tae keep it well fired.

Q. But you said this place was separate from where

you were. Where was it?
A. Away doon the fit o the road. Further doon, in the same buildin.
Q. Were you ever in any other pottery?
A. Ah wis never in oanywhere else, only there. Ah left hit tae go tae munitions.
Q. Which would be about 1914 or so?
A. Oh aye. 16 mebbe.
Q. And what did you call the place?
A. They callit it the "spongin hoose".
Q. But what did you call the whole pottery?
A. We jist cried it "the pottery". "Where div ye work?" "Ah work in the pottery".
Q. Was there only the one pottery?
A. Aye there wis jist the wan pottery in thae days. It wis in Finnieston Street. That's a Ah can tell ye Tony.
(Mrs. McGovern now identifies various pieces of tranfer printing and spongeware from the Verreville site).
Q. Did you cut your own sponges, or did somebody else do this for you?
A. Naw, naw. They gave you the sponge cut.
Q. So they had some people who designed the sponges?
A. Aha. We never cut the sponge - (referring to a piece) - that's no glost yet.
Q. And how long would the sponge last?
A. Oh, a coupla years, mebbe less, say a year.
Q. And how many people would work in the sponging shop with you?
A. Oh well, about 20.
Q. And how many worked in the transfer shop?
A. Weel Ah don't know - Ah think about a dozen.
Q. And how many do you think worked in the whole pottery, taking everybody into account? A hundred?
A, Oh no, less than 100.
Q. Did they have a show room where they could show their wares?
A. Yes, in the gilding shoap they showed off their stuff. Well, mebbe no in the gildin shoap, Ah'm tellin a lie. In a showroom. Jist as ye entered. Ye entered the gate and went up a stairway.
Q. And did they employ salesmen?
A. Aye.
Q. And do you remember if any went abroad to foreign countries?
A. Oh aye. A lot went abroad. Ah wisnae in that line, Tony.
Q. Can you describe what a painted piece was like?
A. Say it was that dish there. You got out the brush an the colour, and what ye were gonna use. Ye worked wi a wee paintbrush.
Q. And there was no pattern on the plate?
A. Naw - you drew it oot.
Q. And can you remember what you painted? Flowers?
A. Aye. They told ye what pattern tae dae.
Q. They did a drawing for you and you copied this onto a plate?
A. Aha.
Q. And can you remember if you painted birds or anything?
A. There was flowers, but ye got animals and birds to paint an a. But no a lot o big birds. They countit up yer dozens, tae see how much ye made. Piecework. They wad count it and it was taken away fae ye. And yer name wis pit oan it.
Q. And you were paid at the end of the week?
A. Iphm. The painting was the highest paid. Hit and the printin shoap. The spongin shoap wasnae as high paid. Hit wis jist wae a sponge.
Q. Did you put your initials on anything you painted, or a number?
A. They took yer name doon, an yer number. Say they wir mine an that - they would be marked up as mine, so they'd know how much tae gie me in a pay.
Q. But would you put your initials on a plate?
A. Naw, jist a number.
Q. You would write that on the plate?
A. Iphm. Jist a wee bit.
Q. And you would put that on anything you painted?
A. Iphm. Anything you did.
Q. So that if anyone would come back at any time in the future, they would know that you had done it?
A. That's right.
Q. So everyone had a number?
A. Aye.
Q, And would you keep that number for all the time you were in the pottery?
A. Oh, aye.
Q. Can you remember your number by any chance?
A. Oh no. Couldnae mind that.
(Then, referring to the tissue paper used in transfer printing wares, and the firing of the wares.)
They went to the kiln house, and wer pitt in abig saigger thing, and pitt intae fire, and then came oot glost.
Q. And how many cups could be put into one sagger, do you think?
A, Oh, half a dozen. Same wi saucers. In different saiggers.
Q. And was the firing a continuous thing?
A. Iphm. It stayed in there so many days to fire up. And they knew when to take them oot. That's what Uncle Paddy did. He took them oot.
That's aboot a Tony.

Index